RAIN KEEPERS

HEARTRENDING TRUE STORIES

SAYAN ROY

Clever Fox® PUBLISHING
Chennai • Bangalore

CLEVER FOX PUBLISHING
Chennai, India

Published by CLEVER FOX PUBLISHING 2026

ISBN: 978-93-7500-721-0

Rain shivers get rain fevers, the fevers from which we are never fully cured. Those fevers leave a memory – those memories change us- rip us.

CONTENTS

Contents

ABOUT THE AUTHOR

Dr Sayan Roy is a university professor and author. Sayan became a bestselling author with his debut novel *Shah Rukh Khan and Winds of Fire* gaining popularity worldwide. The unexpected success of the first book pushed him to write with more air and sincerity- it gave him the courage to tell stories that are strange but true. Absolute heart-cutters and thought benders, the spine-chilling tales tear open the tenets of strange, dark realities that bear upon his massive works of creative non-fiction. Sayan's stories reek of horror and truth that shakes the pillars of belief, taking readers to core of darkness where forces yield, soul shatters. Most of them drawn from true events, rivet new winds of fear and wonder, creating a serenade of happy, sad rousing emotions – even everlasting memories. The author's popular books are available on Amazon, Kobo and across bookstores.

Author's Official Instagram handle: @_author.drsayan

ALSO FROM THE AUTHOR

Shah Rukh Khan and Winds of Fire

Strength - Poetry for Lonely Times

PREFACE

My books have been sold - that thrillingly made me happy! But the day my poems sold - that day - that thing, catapulted my thinking to a more self-inflicted realisation of my true self. I realised I could actually make ends meet, and that made me write with more truth, more sincerity, enduring all other things, obliterating torrents of despair, the sadness it brings!

I believe true writers must be able to endure a lot, everything within and beyond. Writing is not just telling of a tale but opening of a soul, it's a gaining of a terrible understanding that realities bend over and over to finally change to something else that becomes self-ridding. Writers must suffer and without suffering, there is no writing. Writing is a diminution of the torture we bear each day. Writing is a crying coming to life, a heart full of horror coming alive! Without truth, without suffering or bleeding, there is perhaps no writing.

The stories in the book are not stories, but blood taken from my life. Over the years, I have known much happiness, I have come across many cruelties – the cruelty I am penning in this book are not mere tales but broad experiences of my racked living. With much desolation created by a cursed living, with much pain bored by my consciousness to return from the grave I have been dwelling – I have taken the torment to make you smile! A plague in my thinking, an outbreak that spread so fast became an agony to me – pushing me off the cliff to eternal darkness! All the tales you read from here come from a dark demolition- a *devastation of myself*!

Layer by layer, I fell into a sadness- a sickness- a dark of eternal fall, plunging myself to abyss- an endless destruction!

TWO ELEPHANTS

The people you see dying in the first years of your life make a dent so deep that nobody in a million years can fill them up. An aunt of mine, the half-mad- the widow, woundingly beautiful with two most winding eyes, told me this story. I- bred in her lap, adored in her shadow, grew up in her paining shade. She told me this story first when I was four, and many times after - it made me laugh mornings and evenings - it had me laughing to pieces. She left a memory so deep in me - a kind of death wistfulness that often comes, telling me I will see her first the day I die.

Two elephants - one black, one white- were playing on a turf. One fell over the other, and the two rolled down a hill! The village men searched for them all day, all night, but the elephants were not found! Common folks, woodsmen, seekers, whoever knew the forest well, went to search the trunk-whooshers, but there was no sign of them anywhere! Everyone in the hamlet started missing the elephants, maybe it was destiny's writing - the two were not to be found! Tired and hopeless, they left the search. One day, after a long time, the villagers saw the elephants coming up the hill - they both looked confused and *Grey*!

THE BEES SÉANCE

Mr Kawade, on returning from Brazil, started emanating his wild wisdom so much that common folks started thinking of him as some mad genius animal expert! Eagles, elephants, emu, eel – there was nothing he did not know about them. Panther, peacocks, pigeons, peanuts – there was nothing unknown to him!

People approached him with different animal problems, and by strange methods like waving a head over the pet's head, ringing a bell on the cat's shoulder, the man would cure them. The man, the expert, the healer even cleaned their auras to keep them off evil spirits! "There are things that can take your animal away. Cursed! dark little things! I tell you!" said Mr Kawade with much conviction. Fortunately, his practice flourished fast! Animal lovers, keepers and owners from far, far lands came in at large numbers. They sat by his feet all day, leaving finally at night after having consumed the most mystical, very hidden, lesser-known things about animals they see every day! He could also talk to them!!

One day, some honeybees flew into Mr Kawade's house. His son and wife started jumping frantically, but he stood still, as calm as a lake. The bees curved in the air, flying in beldam, spreading out, coming to a point! The venomous colony circled his son first, then his wife, who started screaming in bee terror! The bees finally came spiralling around Mr Kawade.

"He knows how to handle the bees. Just an old Brazilian trick!" he thought and smiled. "With absolute focus held in the mind's eye, the bees cannot do anything."

The bees darted towards Mr Kawade, but he kept his ground. He did not move- stir at all! He did not even blink- his pupils arrested in a spinning gyral as if held by some arcane, most unknown superpower!! The bees came in and flew past him, rushing out of the window! Mr Kawade was still smiling but with pain - a bee from the back had stung him badly – he forgot to *focus* on it!

THE SYCAMORES

Valeria lived in a small village in Spain. She had a couple of friends with whom she spent most of her evenings. One of them was Alejandra and the other one was Camilla. The three would sit sometimes in the bamboo garden, sometimes in the bushes – talking their hearts out, watching the flowers and the sun. Valeria, Alejandra and Camilla had many things in common; they liked the same flowers, the same fruits, even the same flies! They watched the moon waning in the nocturnal sky, paddling their legs in the brown pondwater. Life passed away beautifully for the three friends. They never left each other's company. They were same in almost all aspects, but one thing that made Valeria different from the rest two was the belief in the existence of ghosts.

"You don't know, but they are there!" said Alejandra.

"You must believe us, Valeria! Forget us, you should not disbelieve in ghosts!" pressed Camilla, nervously.

"And why should not I?" Valeria burst out laughing.

"Because they get angry?" said Alejandra with fearfully stricken eyes, touching the cross on neck.

"Ha, Ha, Ha! Look at your face. Ha, Ha, Ha!" Valeria could not stop her laughter! Her finger pointed at Alejandra's face. Then, flicking Camilla's forehead, who sat on her other side, she said, "There is nothing like ghosts or evil or demons!"

“You should not say like that,” said Alejandra, touching her cross again.

“You must not say like that,” repeated Camilla.

Valeria still could not control her laughter but due to some residual respect she had maintained for her dear homies, she sealed her lips! Her eyes though peeked out, chortling.

That night, the three blood-giver pals holding hands under the blood-moon of the dark forest, returned stealthily to their homes.

The forest started from Valeria's backyard, and she was the one who insisted Camilla and Alejandra to come sit by irky, rugged trees! Most nights, she would herself watch the uninhabited tree-land through the crooks of her broken window. Valeria did go to the church, but she was not that attached to God like Camilia or Alejandra. Since their childhood, she has been fighting with them regarding the existence of ghosts! She never could understand whether anything so elusive, dark and incredible like demons could exist!

One deep blue evening, Ajendra and Camilla stared at Valeria, who was gazing at the cotton balls rolling down in the floaty air as if there were invisible stairs midair! They did not just look at her! It was a deep stare!! They both smiled at each other, which Valeria did not see. Then, quickly changing to serious, Camilla said, “Valeria, we found a place!”

“What?!” Valeria looked at her as if falling from the invisible stairs.

“Yes, we found a place!” confirmed Alejandra.

“What place?” Valeria's face changed colour when she understood what her bloodpals were talking about!

Alejandra, Valeria and Camilla kept looking at each other for a while. The cotton balls fell all over the green grass. In the night, in the evening of night! The cross rows- the very perpetual cross row of trees looked unkind and fiendish! The three looked around frightfully and then stared back at each other.

"Where is this place?" Valeria broke the silence first.

"We have already been there, Camilla and I," informed Alejandra.

"What!" said Valeria, a tinge of disbelief in her eyes.

"Yes, we went there last week. It is behind the wetland. It is where the bald cypress ends and the sycamores start," said Camilla.

Valeria took her eyes off Alejandra, placing them on Camilla.

"The ghost trees!" sprang up Valeria from her place.

"What? Are you scared of the sycamores?" asked Camilla, the sly smile returned to the nook of her eyes.

"No…," Valeria stood her ground. She became nervy. She said, "But nobody goes there."

"But we have been. We both have been there!" Alejandra said and smilingly looked at Camilla who also smiled.

"What do you two want?" a blotch of sweat ran spattering on Valeria's forehead.

"To come with us," answered Camilla.

"Okay, I will go, but this better not be any of your brain-rot dim pranks!!" said Valeria, angry now.

"That's like our brave friend Valeria. Always a lot of valour!" said Alejandro, sardonically. Camilla patted Valeria's shoulder.

The next day the three friends set out for the secret place in the late evening. First, they crossed the peonies, then the birches, then the nook as they strolled deeper into the dark of the forest, the moon lit more cruelly over their heads! No wind, just the hissing of snakes and unknown sounds of anonymous beasts! All the way, a pensive worry has had Valeria, but she chose not to reveal her angst to her blood-allies. She remained silent so did the other two. Their shadows elongated in the bare protrusions of cypress knees coming out of the water like bony appendages. A moonbeam paining, lonely and separating, fell on the needle-lost branches of bald cypress growing like hands on the dim wetland! A grey fog flew all over - Valeria's heart pounded fast, but she did not express any of this to her friends.

When they reached the backside of the marsh where the moon fell blatantly on the white sycamores, they clasped each other's hands tight! A feeling of dread is devouring their insides!! Pale, bloodless, breathless, the ghost trees crooked towards the white moon, the forest dead black frightened a bending dark!

Alejandro and Camilla went to a nook while Valeria waited alone on the black land. She stood there alone, pinning the fear of the place. The more she channelled the fearsome place, the more she felt lonely, broken, lost in the macabre realm! The black wind is talking to her ears, something is walking there!! With evil thoughts shallowing her down, Camilla and Alejandro returned with a stone.

"What is this?" asked Valeria.

"A marsh stone!" said Alejandro.

"Take out your hand," said Camilla.

"Why?" asked Valeria, her face red with confusion, a fear stabbing her continuously.

"Just give your hand," demanded Alejandro, her eyes mean.

Valeria held her composure, thought something and straightened her hands.

Suddenly, Camilla took out a dagger and ran it shamelessly across Valeria's veins.

"What the hell are you doing?!" bellowed Valeria, her eyes red with fury.

Suddenly Camilla's face changed to a playful smile, she said, "Look at your hand, you fool! It is just a small cut!"

"She is just playing with you, broke-head! She knows her arts!" said Alejandro.

Valeria looked at her hand. They were right, it was indeed a small cut.

"Now, Valeria, listen to us carefully!" said Camilla, her eyes most terribly lit. "We will put your blood in this marsh stone and say Espíritu three times! Whatever it is. It will come for you!"

"Really?" said Valeria coldly.

"We are not joking, Valeria, you sure you want to do this?" asked Alejandro.

The three stood there in the dark, rotten swamp of dark times, in a darkness pleading to be released!

"Yes!" said Valeria.

Camilla and Alejandro's faces turned pale with fear. They could not believe their ears. Unsure if the legend was true, unsure what to say, they kept looking at Valeria!

"Go ahead! Do it!" said Valeria, extending her hands. "Take my blood!"

"Don't be naïve, Valeria. It can be dangerous," said Alejandro, her eyes terrified.

"No. I want to do this. You all have bogus beliefs. There is nothing like evil," Valeria remained persistent.

Unwilling, Camilla took some blood from Valeria's hand and put it on the marsh stone. The cracks on it sucked the blood inside.

All three of them chanted *Espirito* three times.

One hour, two hours, three hours, waiting in the black marshland, the three pals became tired. Nothing happened. While coming back, Camilla and Alejandro looked thoughtful, while Valeria stopped and giggling.

Three days have passed, Valeria is now sitting on a wooden chair, most wretched, she is looking at the marsh stone. The stone is usual, only that it is taking hands and legs. She has tried throwing it away, but it has come back. She does not like eating, and she does not like drinking. All she wants is to look at the tall trees and think of the bald moon light, the lost sycamores! Alejandra and Camilla have died a disfigured death. The death that only peers but does not come to her. Writhing and hungry, she waits!

Four days have passed. She is now looking at herself in a mirror! She looks the oldest, frighteningly old! Her skin decayed- eyes drooping, her breathing laboured!! She cannot sleep. She cannot be awake! The thing whose hideous black face curves out its red lips keeps visiting her! Straws in a Hessian sack form the head of a standing creature, a brute unspeakable thing, a pure evil!!

"You two put me in a labyrinth. A cruel labyrinth that goes nowhere!" Tears fell from her olden wrinkled eyes.

Eighth day. She thought of the cruel trees, the night that killed the moon. What she is looking at now is the most bedevilled thing. The marsh stone is not a stone anymore; it has grown. It stands now on its feet, it has two hands, two hands stretching out! It is a Scarecrow, a monstrous black face coming closer to her!

MORBID TREASURE

Five men gathered on a bridge. Tonight is the night they must get the work done. A box of gold, a diamond-studded sword, a runic jewel of dark ages - together they are worth millions! According to a source, all these priceless objects lie hidden underground behind the one-thousand-year-old ruined church! The five men stealthily walked past the houses draped in stygian black of a monsoon night. Black clouds brewed in the dark, making the little air of the strange night damp, even more alone! All houses were locked, all chaps slept deep!

Reaching, they broke the lock of the moth-eaten church gate. Then, carefully walking under the tall trees of an unknown past, they reached the backyard. Worms, critters and hives left the place morbid and monstrous! It was not for any living to dwell there - nobody but the deep night stood alone sleeping in the black graveyard!! One of the five crooks held all the supplies while the other four started to dig. Four spades in lightning-fast motion dug up a whole lot of ground in a short time. They found bones and worms - the bats and the owls gawked at them! The grey wind turning black came flying to them, murmuring to their greed- their heart of sins! A timepiece ticked, a woman laughed, some shadows chuckled, the eyeless passed by! The five men saw none, heard nobody; they kept digging, burrowing arduously! They will be rich, very rich. Only some more soil- some black, dead soil of a dead graveyard, and the treasure will be theirs!

Digging to a state of half-dead hollow, the treasure lurked in the morbid land revealed itself! Zeal in their eyes when they found the treasure!! *The legends were true* - a box of shining gold, a sword in shimmering white diamonds, a gem even rarer and stranger, all together, all perfectly made on a buried painting!

LAUGHING KINGDOM

A blacksmith was accused of making bent swords. "Why are the swords curved?" This was everybody's question. The tidings of the blacksmith making crooked swords spread out like fire in the kingdom. Soon, he was summoned to the King's court.

"The swords you made are all bent! Because of you, we lost the battle!" shouts the knight, seeing the timid blacksmith entering the courtroom.

"Jajaja," laughs the people in the court!

"Oh, the fool!" jibes the king.

"Jajaja," laugh the people in the court!

"Oh, the master!" mocks the bishop.

"Jajaja," laugh the people in the court again!!

"The hero of our loss, maker of bent swords!" added the priest in a sly tone.

Again, the people laughed loudly, "Jajaja, Jajaja!" They were happy; the blacksmith was being shown his place. Many urged that the king and the ministry should immediately punish the blacksmith for his unforgivable blunder. "How can he be this silly? What blacksmith makes curved swords?" they asked. "Punish him now! Kill him now," they demanded, throwing stones at the blacksmith. They laughed and hooted and called him by different names, "Half-wit"! "Silly"! "Sword bender"! and whatnot!

The blacksmith watched everything with silent eyes. A dozen stones hit him too! Little blood dripped down from his head, but he kept quiet. He stood alone. An affliction most disheartening- very unspeakable of, a conscience most self-piteous and self-losing made him fall on his knees! The throwers kept laughing at him; they never stopped throwing! The row of laughter, "Jajaja Jajaja Jajaja" flew around like bats in the sad, ill court. Devious it sounded- lacerating it was to him! He, a scoundrel, ,the ill-omened, kept gaping at the laughing mass. "Bent swords, curved swords!" they kept mocking him, tearing his soul apart. The blacksmith, with head bent, knees bent, hailed before the king. Keeping his eyes still on the ground, softly he said, "But those are bows!"

The people there suddenly stopped their laughter. The king, the knight, and the priest of Fool's kingdom stopped their laughter too. Instead, they started gawking at each other!!

SONJA

All day long she plays – her name is Sonja. "Sonja! Sonja! Sonja!" her mother bangs her head on the door, floor, chair and walls - the munchkin never listens to her! Sonja has two tigers, one frog and a doll which she keeps carefully in her old cooking pot. Last summer, her mother gave her this special silver container with thirteen crooked holes, nine scratches, seven bents and many burn marks- hence unfit for cooking! She doted on her stuffies and animal heads very much! She never liked having a friend. Selfish self-play! That's all – that was her aim, to play all day alone! Due to his carefree and careless attitude she received three smacks each day, three tight slaps right-and-left from her un-dear, unwanted mother! A thousand times has she not told Sonja- a complete urchin- to eat and sleep on time! And how many times did Sonja listen to mum? None! Why should Sonja care? She is busy playing. Whenever she was called between her play or she saw people coming to break her play, the imp got vexed! Yes, that one thing that fumed out of her little nose day-night-evening-dawn was anger! Her mother suffered a great deal due to this bad temper of hers! 'Bad, bad Sonja!' she would call her!

One day, after having combed the doll's hair one hundred thirty-three times perpetually in single monotony, Sonja felt hungry. As usual, without calling her mother or telling her so, she started crying! Nobody came. She kept crying! Minutes passed. She kept crying! The clock arm on the teddy's head fell. She kept crying! Nobody came. Getting no answer, the oceans stopped flowing from her eyes! The little urchin at will could control it- the tears! Sonja got up, holding her hungry belly and peeped into the kitchen.

'Oh, there is mother!' Sonja got angry as she saw her sitting. She brushed her very long frock along the ground and hurried to her mother, only to find her playing with the same toys as her!

PICKING LILLIES

Told by her who died untreated in a hospital, this story remained like a spark in me all these years. I, who will love her at any cost - my beloved Masi holding whose hands I ran the green fields, in whose love my entire childhood passed.

A little girl was picking up lilies by the pond. Red, yellow, and white all lilies grew there! As she walked, more lilies sprang up as if a band of fairies had come in at night and planted them everywhere. The lilies were painfully beautiful!

The lass picked them one by one and put them into her little basket. As she went closer to the pond, the sea of lilies started to appear bigger. She started picking them up too, the big lilies- especially the big beautiful white ones!! She picked the lilies from the water too, the pretty water lilies! The day looked like a dream - sun shades and shadows elongated like festoons in losing hours of midsummer noon!! Lillies were in every nook, every rook- it was Lilies Day! Picking lilies, she saw some frogs leaping into the pond. A lot of frogs - green, dark green, yellow, blue frolicking, rollicking and leaping into the pond. First, she did not understand what was going on. Then she saw it - she was not picking lilies anymore, those were mushrooms!

PERIL RIVER

Satish sat on a boat and sailed into the river. The tides picked up, and the moon smiled bright in the night sky! He prayed to all nineteen gods and goddesses he knew of. He even prayed to the unknown god of river, whom he had heard from the fisherman, to be extremely powerful! The tides rising and becoming mountains came down like a Herculean crossbow of lightening carnage! Terrified, he closed his eyes and continued praying with the honest fear that sparked up fountains of fear inside his fragile ribcage! He prayed, prayed and prayed, and then there was a *miracle!* When he opened his eyes, he was sitting on his bed, the early morning sun freckling down its slanting rays, the old window never looked so beautiful before!

THE TREE-HOLE

A cold, frosty winter covered the crops and huts of Hamna. The grass failed to grow, the water ceased to flow, the faces did not glow. The villagers with little food and little hope - got worried. The clan master paced up and down in his hut. They have not worshipped the tree-hole for a week! Little they could do too, the tree-hole was in the north frontier of the village before which lay large blocks of ice and frosted giant rocks. Nobody could get there.

The tree-hole was a round opening in a pine bark. The villagers believed it to be sacred - it was home to their village's Goddess Lisha. Not worshipped, the Goddess unleashed a curse, a curse most terrible – the curse of blue winter!

"Something must be done!" demanded the clan master.

"Yes, master, but how do we get there?" asked the tree-surgeon.

"Get the huntsmen to work, take as many men as you want, but find a way," commanded the old master.

"We need new tools, stronger tools," urged the blacksmith from the corner.

"Weld the best metals, yield the finest axes," ordered the clan master.

Heavy axes were made. New spades were forged. Desperate, the huntsmen and tree-surgeons cut down all the snow blocks and rocks. Bodies of birds and animals that died in fierce frost famine were put aside. The region was cleared. A new road was made.

Walking about a mile on the road, the sacred tree was finally seen. It was clad with snow.

"There!" shouted one of the men, pointing towards the tree.

A dead silence circled the frozen tree. No moths, no ants, not even a fly hovered nearby. Only some resin dripped- fell quietly, lonely spider webs hung around its snow-eaten branches.

All the people of Hamna followed him and gathered in front of the tree. The old clan master walked up to the sacred tree and placed a bowl of fruits in the round tree-hole. The village shaman came near and offered a quick prayer to the pine tree. Then, the shaman closed his eyes and entered a seance. Communicating with the tree spirit for a while, he slowly came out of it.

"We must all close our eyes now," announced the shaman.

"Yes, let us all close our eyes for the offering," repeated the clan master.

The people of Hamna did exactly what they were told - they closed their eyes and drew three circles in the air, mumbling some secret words!

While the offering was made, a little girl left her father's hand and ran to the tree-hole. Picking the wooden bowl up, she began to eat the fruits. Greed in her eyes, pangs in her gut, months she had not eaten properly!

Seeing her munch the apples and pears, all the villagers shrieked with fear. Angry and fuming, the clan master seized the bowl from the girl.

"How dare you touch this sacred bowl, Claudia?" shrieked the clan master. "The Goddess will never forgive us! We are doomed," his cloudy eyes praying mercy.

But the bowl was empty. The fruits were gone, so was the blue winter!!

THE LOST HERD

The herd had seven goats, four cows and three sheep. It was a unique, rich herd that the village folks had ever seen! They wandered on their own on their own little farm!! The farm owner sprinkled his life on them, but one night, they all got lost! The farm owner got very worried. He sent men to search for his beloved animals! They searched for the stock throughout the village! They raided the wine shop, the slaughter house, the grocery shop, the witchdoctor's hut, they rummaged everywhere! But the gummers were not found! The farm owner was a rich man. The herd was costly! It cost him quite a lot. Anybody could have stolen them. "But how come all the animals, every cow, every goat, every sheep goes missing in the same night?" The thought never left the farm owner, "Somebody already had eyes on my poor little animals! He really had planned this well!! Sooner or later, I will catch him!"

Days passed, weeks passed, and the owner became tired of searching.

'They are costly. They are very precious!' shouted the rich farm owner sitting in a nearby police station. "You must find them. You must catch that imbecile thug!"

The police sent their men too. They searched for the herd full-heartedly. More days and weeks passed, but the herd was not found. The farm owner began to shrink in sorrow! A violent sorrow took him over! A defeating gloom entered him! He did not leave his bed. He did not leave his house. He remained there, sitting all day in one armchair, looking out towards the farm! "My farm, my animals!" he often cried at night, "The lush green farm empty, empty!"

A deep, profuse sadness ate him every day. A rush of pain came winding from inside – that tore him each day! He thought of his lost cattle, the lost moments and a wistfulness so rogue churned him inside out! He died a little each day! He left eating, he left drinking. The doctors came and went back. Nobody could do anything. He grew thinner and thinner. "Oh! My poor animals! They must be starving somewhere!" he bashed his head against the wood. A sadness so grievous possessed him that even the villagers became worried about him. They wished for his recovery. They searched for his animals, but nobody could find his herd.

One night when the farm owner was sleeping, he heard some noises. He lit up a taper and rested his feet on the cold ground. Then, with weak steps, he made way to the heavy door. Waddling, when he reached the door that opened to the night farm, he saw something! The stars blinked above the cows mowing, the sheep baaing and the goats bleating! He was amazed- thrilled! All his dear steers and bucks were peacefully eating their grass. They were there- standing right in front of his eyes! It was like a dream- a pure dream! Then his eyes fell on the farm gate. Somebody was leaving. His eyes clumsy and sleepy could not believe what he was seeing – a tall, shadowy man- he had no body! A black foggy figure, darker than the night!

ROLI'S TEARS

Roli's mother was cutting vegetables in the kitchen. Roli woke up with teary eyes, the briny waters spilling down her sweet face! Every morning, for having to suffer these insufferable onion tears, Roli disliked her mother (very much!).

"Has Roli woken up?" mused her mother, dotingly.

"Yes, by your onions?" replied Roli sourly, her eyes full of childish disappointment for not having completed her morning's sleep. She sounded cranky- also silly!

"The onions! Oh, these?" said the mother, snapping her finger on the sharp cutter.

In a jiffy, Roli's onion tears turned to real tears. She ran to her mother's rescue. She helped her clean the wound and applied a bandage.

"Mama, the onion soup you make is delicious. I love it, but please be careful!" The fear was real in her eyes.

Her mother nodded, she said, 'My little Roli has grown up, hasn't she?"

BLACK WOODS

Esteban, tired and depleted, kept walking. He has been walking for days but he could not get where he should have been by now – a forest. He was a hunter after all! He killed animals and birds, and that's all he did. Call it pleasure, a hobby or a transfer of royal genes from his royal ancestors, who he thought were kings. Trees, wilderness, the forest nights, the moments of silence before the killing excited him! Esteban would not think twice before taking another man's life if they told him to quit hunting! He was not just a hunter. He was a murderer too.

"Hunting is in our blood, animals fear us," he would often boast, cleaning his rifle, which to him was the same as ancestral gold. "Oh! Don't be a coward. There is nothing to fear animals," he often told his friends. Some did accompany him, but shaken by his merciless streak of killing animals, they avoided the dark venture from next time.

This time too, he has come to visit a forest, a forest most dark and rending to every step taken. Beliefs most strange, thoughts most mysteriously dark and fearsome have been linked to this forest where Esteban headed to. Eight days and nine nights, he is still on trails to these woods where legend has lived the most sinister things, creatures that suck blood and empty leaves, leaving not a fragment of shredded bone! Walking another three hundred yards, Esteban found a river most distasteful, marshy and pungent! From the other side of it, a forest most black and hidden. Something was strange. Not even a speck of light entered the most shadowy forest he had ever seen.

He built a raft all by himself. It cost him the day's light, but it was well-built. When he crossed the river to reach the woodland, it was midnight. The shadows of the sinister dark fell all over the wild place. Not a sound, not even a bug there! Just a silence, a perfect silence that cannot be understood, that cannot be broken – lived there. The wind was crossing, cutting him and entering the forest but the wind had no sound too – strange! Everything, the forest, the trees, the bees, the hives, all lay hushed in a spell of eternal sadness. The trees monstrous and harrowing crooked had the most curved branches - Esteban spellbound kept looking at them. For the very first time in his whole life, in the half-moon light of a bloody night, his feet shivered! The hunter, always very valiant and violent, who did not fear anything, now standing at the edge of a strange wild where the moon shone lonely in the only corner of the diabolic woodland, thought, "It will be better to go in when the sun comes out."

Then, behind a hidden rock, keeping his rifle beside him, he lay down. However, moments before sleep when memories cross a blurry reality, he felt the place with all his senses – the more he felt, the more he felt blocked out as if somebody from somewhere did not let him in! A feeling so dark and evil that a person as cruel as Esteban felt the fear of it!

The next day when he woke up, the sun flakes fell across his face- the wild river flowing. He cleaned himself in the river water, not going too deep. There were crocodiles, man-eating fishes and whatnot! Esteban decided not to waste a bullet on these petty things. He has killed them enough.

When he entered the forest, the first thing he saw was the barks – the barks and the branches of the old, odd trees, most contorted, twisted and mortifying – leaving a leaf of sadness nailed hanging in the air. The spirit of the forest, if anything had remained of it, was very sad; the wind carried a soul of sadness, like someone's weeping! A strange mystic wildland of emptiness – the more the huntsman walked, the more the feeling of desolation, of someone crying, someone leaving never to return, returned to him again and again – caught him deep! The feeling was so hard and hollowing that it cut through Esteban – slowing him down.

Coming to a marsh, he found a tree with the most charming fruits one could ever see! His mouth started watering, and as soon as he took a bite of one lovely fruit, he found it to be hollow and rotten! Stunned, Esteban checked the other ones. To a strange oblivion of a maddening perplexity – he found all of them to be hollow, all of them to be rotten as if something, suddenly, had drawn life out of them! They did not even get the time to die!

Thirsty and hungry, Esteban kept walking. The tendrils, the vines, the long roots dropping down from the strangely long crooked trees called him near. Their deformed branches hovered over him to see who had come! Esteban kept the rifle close. Anytime, if anything appears, he must shoot right away! He was prepared.

Esteban kept walking until his feet were unable to push blood anymore, his whole body came to a sudden halt. He fell on his knees and in front of him, stood a wooden cabin, most uncanny, old and secretive. It was an ash grey cabin, it looked abandoned! The woods, winds, and seeds all grey in a gloomy grey of a cloudy day. The place was empty, lifeless and cold on a lifeless day. The strange, sad feeling of somebody left roused his shards of his flesh!

He stood up and dragged his feet a bit near! The place, the boughs and the burrows looked older. To his strange discovery, he found some bones – bones white and long, bones that were not of human. Esteban took a few bones in his hand and in a moment, he understood whose those were of! Cows and buffaloes! The bones still had fresh stains of blood on them but no flesh around. 'But who could have eaten these large animals with such savage cruelty?' thought the ruthless killer. He got afraid, the feeling of a strange loneliness rode stronger – he looked at the cabin, the dark grey cabin. Even in the twisted lanes of his cruel heart, Esteban felt a desolation so sharp and distinct, like nobody has anybody in this world, everything is ruined, doomed to destruction!

The hunter left the bones and made his way towards the cabin. Reaching the porch, he found an armchair very old and dusty lying. 'Somebody used to live here!' the hunter thought, stepping into the cabin. The black door rusted and blackened with webs had no spider's webbing – life looked untrue, suddenly again the weeping of sadness, the melancholic wind of emptiness, awakening rue eating him inside! He stared at the left bones so mercilessly severed from the heads, a body that left no corpse! He felt terrorized but with all his fear pushing along, he threw the cabin door open. There was nothing inside!

Esteban in an unknown cabin of an unknown forest in the dying rays of last daylight, was standing in a room that had no furniture, no lights, no paint on the wall, the walls opened like veins of a dead carcass, a black cabin with a world of blackness inside. Everything seemed grey and black, dark and untrue!

The darkness fell outside. Esteban sat down in the empty cabin. He decided to pass the night there.

He may have well fallen asleep when a soft clatter of things woke him up. There was no moon in the sky, just a faint hint of some light coming from somewhere, which shook him up! 'Somebody may be inside the house!', a bleak, cold blowing outside, the wind whispering sorrowful like someone crying rushed through the night! Cold and lonely, he felt dozy.

The dim light made a circular ring on the wall- the strange circle, half lit, half hazy on the blank wall was clawed, which meant the light could only shine through the cracks of wooden planks on which he was sitting! He shuddered with fear. It was meant someone was underneath him!

Esteban stood up, his ears blood-awake like nails of a vicious animal. He knew whatever it was, it has come! It has come in search of him!!

He held his breath and choosing his steps silently like a predator, he went outside- the night with all its might laid hollow, morose and sinister! All the hair in Esteban's body raised up, he started looking for the secret path which led the *thing* to the secret chamber underneath! 'Whatever that thing is! It will not see tomorrow's daylight!' a violent rage of galling barbery broke open in his ruthless veins. The hunter went to the backyard, where he found a tunnel dug open. Creeping into it stealthily, he kept the gun pointed at the front!

As he crawled through the tunnel, a smell of dead and decayed flesh blinded his senses. Crawling through the narrow, loose hollow, his body stiffened with blood, he dreaded profusely. He is in depth, he is in ruthless killing of all creatures have always kept his dare burning, but this strange night, a second wave of painful petrification has fought against his passion. He could not help feeling a writhing sadness of someone crying somewhere- a fear, too! He opened his ears even more keenly and pressed them against the cold tunnel mud. Esteban heard something! And with a lurch, he realised the weeping he had been imagining so long was not an imagination after all! It was real, it was true!! It was now coming from where the ghastly lamp had been lit. Many sins, many things merciless and cruel committed, he has never been defeated. Then why should he stop tonight?!

As an ant with wings flies to the flame to die, the heartless murderer kept crawling and crawling till he reached the end of the heinous passage. He jumped out of his stealth into the underground chamber lit by a thousand candles. Dolls torn, cut human and animal heads lay scattered on all sides, a night most fierce and satanic curdled his blood over - the killer in him loose unleashed! In a flash, all his excitement was wiped out like thinning wax of a dying candle – his face turned cold blue, all his morsels hardened. The faint ripple of someone weeping sorrowfully came sailing to his ears. It was coming from another chamber behind! With rending thirst of hounding, he walked between the bodyless heads spattered on the ground, stained with blood to the end-room. Reaching, he found the room to be dark, a blue dark everywhere; there was no candle, nothing! In the corner, then he saw something, a shadowy mirror, in front of it sat someone combing! His soul left his remains; his lungs choked when he saw her! A woman with hair touching her feet sat there, combing in the black mirror! Her face white and shredded, her eyes lonely black, nothing in it – just the endless streaks of black tears ran down from her tenebrous eyes! Crying, bending her hand and contorting herself on the floor, weeping through abandoned black eyes – she came to Esteban! And then, a wind-breaking shriek of someone dying in sadistic brutality broke through the eaten hollow barks of the abandoned black woods!!

BINTI LOVES BINTI

Both looked the same, same face, same eyes, same smile, same! Same! One was a boy, the other was a girl. Both their nicknames were Binti! Little faces, cuddly bairns, Binti and Binti were brother and sister!

Binti and Binti lived with their parents, and both were awfully mischievous. Days when brother Binti did not feel like going to school, sister Binti sat in his class. The teacher could not recognise her! Days when sister Binti did not feel like going to school, brother Binti sat in her class. The teacher could not recognise him either!

The same mischiefs started happening at home - on dinner tables, in prayer rooms, on festival times - the parents, relatives, neighbours, nobody could tell the difference! Sometimes they played pulling each other's hair- a play that would fast change to a vicious episode of vendetta hair pulling- heavy crying! The parents scolded the wrong child, always! This, too, on their own fault- pique their ire - they always beat up the wrong urchin!

Irked in the ruckus of two little sprogs, the parents sat heads in hands! Still, the gossamer gust of their joyful childhood days passed by. Brother and sister took great care of each other. Brother Binti helped sister Binti in chores, sister Binti helped brother Binti in studies. Whether tying of hair or taking sister Binti to school, brother Binti always stood up as a protective brother. Whenever her brother fell sick, sister Binti fed him oatmeal like a doting sister. Soon, all the parents' ire changed to pride; everybody said, 'Binti loves Binti very much.'

THE SECRET

Somebody stands outside the north window, watching Mina sleep in the shadows of lambent moonshine. It does not move, blurry and hidden it remains in the shadows. Every night, it comes and watches her sleep. Tonight, she too kept looking at what was looking at her from behind the dark curtains- the night more awake than other nights! She knew it would come for her; she knew everything! *The song of blood* rose in her ears, coming back from former nights of dying frights. Ailed by a terrible curse, a disease has writhed her nerves and body – she lay still on her bed, her heart fluttering in loneliness of the dark, roue night. Some nights are hollow from inside - they come as shadows only. Sick and pale, Mina saw death nearing!

But before dying, she had to try it once. She got up from bed and drifted in a aria of sadness, the blood song rustling to her ears. She knew things nobody else did. She had it burning inside her – a secret! The time has come for it to be revealed. She has no other choice!

Lighting a votive candle, she awaited midnight. Terrified seeing the spectre appearing again, Mina took the candle's molten wax in her thumb and pressed it in the middle of her forehead. First, nothing happened. Then, she pressed harder. She kept pressing until her whole life, her whole life memories and existence would be forced into her forehead! The night changed shadows, the face that was lurking before was not hiding anymore, maybe it understood what Mina was trying to do! Mina's thumb curved backwards, causing a terrible pain, her ears tinging! The face came a few yards closer. It was standing inside the room now- watching Mina with red blood-soaked eyes! She kept pressing writhingly until something very cold spiralled up her spine, only to arch out of her body – a flying Urn which hurried into the horrid, shadowy face to capture it! Mina opened her eyes, her countenance flushed with fear, her thumb almost broken! She saw the grisly red, the urn wings and another one-eyed woman's face disappearing in the thin air!

Mina fell on the ground. When she woke up, it was a beautiful evening! Children were playing on the green riverside, the moon tilting over windbreaker palms. She stood up; she felt weak for not having eaten properly for days. Hungry, she grabbed a crab apple and the moment she went to take a bite, she was astounded by what she saw in the mirror! She was twenty again, young and beautiful! The secret has worked. The *Age Keeper* has been vanquished! He will come back again after a hundred years.

THE CRYING WIFE

A wife, after fighting with her husband, cried an ocean! She took a ship and sailed away. The husband came searching for his wife. Walking a mile or two, he found an ocean. Finding no ship, he started to swim. The huge waves bulged in, the sun rays rolled- the nights passed but he kept swimming. Hungry, terrified, he hung on to his heart. The winds wave by the nights of storms sung by. The seagulls flew by, but he kept going – in search of her whom he loved the most. 'Life is so uncertain, a life so loved so unloved suddenly. A life so blissful, so cursing!!' he thought.

A week passed like this. He became tired- tired of swimming. He cried at last when he could not find her!

On the eighth day, he was so exhausted he could swim no more. He closed his eyes and waited for the waters to gulp him. Seeing her husband dying, the wife became sad, she stopped crying and the oceans dried up. When the man opened his eyes, he was lying on a vast stretch of land. The land was dry. His wife was sitting beside him, smiling.

AUNT MADELINE

"Can you see the stars blinking, Aunt Maddie?" asked the boy in the yellow birthday hat.

Four stars in the black sky lay in silence like the tail of a sleeping constellation. The town merged with the starry night looked like a dream, waving from a far-reaching starry world. The boy, oddly dressed in a Christmas costume, disturbed by the day's playing and running around, kept looking at the night sky - it was magic curled in winters like a hand-painted all the yellow stars blinking, stirring, rolling in the Christmas sky. Then his eyes fell on the streets, and for a moment, he was petrified. Then, after gulping a couple of air bubbles stuck in his papery throat, he said, "Can you see them, aunty? They are on the streets, right under the stars!"

He was staring at a group of women holding hands; they all had scarves on, and they all had tall, thin candles grasped in their hands. They were speaking something continually, very fast. The boy standing and stirring on his feet, several storeys above could hear their mumblings! He could not make out anything he was hearing, his eyes transfixed on the women in the dark corner of the road, the candles now pointed towards him!

Not a moment was to be wasted, Madeline, hearing what she had heard, rushed to the room. Pushing aside Joseph, she ran to close the windows. She kept her eyes tightly closed while shutting the panes – she did not want to see what she was made to see!

"How many times have I told you not to open these windows?" she yelled, in a maddening fit of benumbing fright. "Don't you know what happened to the boys and girls in our locality. They have been coming and taking the children away. Don't you know that? God forbid if anything happens to you! I can't even think..."

She could not finish her line, the windows which she just closed were shut alright. But the room was dark – dark as hell! She felt empty, very empty, like the world had been sucked out of her. In that moment of stygian loneliness feeding the cloisters of her empty soul, she felt a fear, a fear most dreadful! The lights came back in a jiffy – her soul teleported back to her body!

But where is Joseph? In his place stood a doll with the face of a large white star, strands of green wool hanging out in place of arms! She went near, and with hands shivering and eyes tearing, she touched the doll. It looked like Joseph but was not Joseph, it was really a doll, a stuffed doll! Madeline ran desperately throughout the house, he searched the rooms, the backyards, the garden, underneath the stairs, in the bathrooms. But there was no sign of Joseph in the house. She ran across the lawn to the gate, opened the gate and went straight to the joint where Joseph had pointed through the windows. The place was mortifying, sad, painfully left- had nobody!

Madeline, crying and huffing, fell flat on his knees, her heart sank in bygone thoughts of his forever loved boy. "They took him too," her mind told her.

THE TENANT

Ajit has been living in this broken house for the last four months – a life without friends and relatives, far away. The house so broken is a part of an even more wrecked palace, a desolate palace with mostly bricks as remnants of it. A dark mist covered its buried rooms and unused kitchens. A large part of the palace was uninhabited, and the only part that was still human – have been the house of the landlord and his family for decades. From the family now, the landlord is the only one alive in this forsaken house! The landlord inhabited the ground floor but was out of the town. The landlord was like a father to Ajit, who treated him well and provided him with aid in times of need. Because the malady of catching breaths makes old age unbearable, one of the landlord's distant brothers has taken him out of town – for a change of air!

The ground floor, shabby, old-looking, full of cobwebs and pigeon-holes, had mountings of various dead animals. Only the room where the old man lived had some plants breathing arduously, facing the shabby windows of faint moonlight. The value of life is felt more when one lives alone with himself, and in the strange wind of the evening, Ajit felt one with the musky dark mist which settled in the November air. The people of this town did not talk much; they worked, they lived peacefully. But since he has come to his town, he has found a life of his own. The broken house, the forgotten palace, had a spirit of dark that intoxicated and enlivened him – he used to forget all his tiredness while being present between its walls.

Ajit found a quiet peacefulness in this palace house. A bliss, a silence, a mutual peace kept blowing in the night air, night after night - every night that follows the dusty, yellow days. Ajit worked in a nearby factory, another place where there is not much light left for life, same old rusted machines, same old blast furnace, same old sounds of metal cutting through metals. After day's work, Ajit spent most of his evenings looking at the wind-beaten terraces of the old locality, which lay side by side, like wings of a mud butterfly. Beneath the iron antennas sat the desolate grave of ancient shops, buried in waves of lost time!

The wrecked palace of the landlord stood still at the last corner of the town, peering behind the bones of collapsed slums and the turbid green of perilous climbers. Adjacent to the back wall of mellowed bricks, a small forsaken garden with one lonely tree survived, which showed no sign of fruits or leaves. Many days, till late in the night, Ajit talked to his parents over the phone; his mother, who has pleaded for his return, spent two precious hours every day complaining about the remote, which won't work at all. 'Family and family things, he echoed to himself as he walked down the winding stairs of the dark, wretched palace. The stairs ended in the shadowy space of the first floor, where they were immersed in a tale of night - the pale portraits of the landlord's ancestors.

Many times, Ajit invited his colleagues over. Once they had drunk together, they spent hours conversing and roaming in the house, but despite having people, they had a certain emptiness – an emptiness that does not leave. An emptiness that only stands and peers!

One evening, Ajit started penning his life diary again while the clatter of the utensils could be heard from the backside kitchen, 'the maid' he knew it. Ajit focused back, flipping pages after pages, scrutinising the thoughts of days lived - thinking of his firelight hometown, his old parents. While flipping, a stroke of wind blew through the curtains, ruffling the pages of the calendar and tilting the oval glass painting, which bore the forgotten colours of the palace, an artist's faded signature dated two hundred and seventy years back!

Foraging on leaves, the almost departed palace, which lives now like a goblin of dead dark, its present-day rib-broken pillars once had the splendour of a king's palace - the green and red windowpanes graced the sun glows into hearth of the courtyard. These mortar walls were alive then, the landlord's ancestors were living - those were the days of horses, lanterns, and myth! "But something in the following decades has happened to the palace, changing its nature completely - something which the painting does not embody but the house carries even now," reflected Ajit, gazing at the painting. Ajit felt a racking pain – a pain of a distinct contrast created by years running between the past and present! 'There is a thing! a thing beyond the understanding of the mundane, a skulked tale which tormented and deformed this aged old house. But what torments the house? What remains in here that renders the house and its surroundings so departed?' the train of thoughts never came to a stop.

One hour of jumbled thoughts passed by when a woman's voice from the back broke his daze, 'Sir, your dinner is ready. I am leaving. Please lock the door."

"Okay, Rohini," Ajit stood up, adding, "Please do not be late tomorrow. I am telling this not for myself, but you have to return home as well. This part of the town is lonely, you know it, and it is not safe at night."

Nodding her head, Rohini walked away. Ajit followed her down the abhorrent, dark stairs in pursuit of the main door, which he must close after she leaves. Rohini, after leaving the house, with quick nervy steps, disappeared into the black mist of the night. Ajit closed the door.

That night, Ajit could not sleep. The lamplight remained as it was by the bedside, the palace remained as desolate as it was. But an uncanny cackle echoed repeatedly back to his pointed ears; he heard it in his sleep. Somebody was screeching!

Over the following few days, Ajit showed some signs of change. He started returning from the factory early, he started strolling more on the night terrace, burned more cigarettes, and started to think more to the verge of overthinking. Through all these unusual changes, all the time Ajit felt as if something rare and buried was calling out to him! Maybe from the past! He felt a connection, most urgent and calling, a connection to something that had lurked in the shadows of centuries. Ajit felt a hysterical desire to discover what remained hidden!

In the next few days, more changes were seen. Ajit would be looking at the lean, listless tree standing leafless and lifeless, while his parents kept calling and calling. Once every two days, he would receive their calls but end the conversations quickly to continue doing what he has been doing – exploring the dark corners of the empty house.

He would even leave his after-work conversations suddenly and saunter back to the desolate house, as if something lonely, hidden whispered to him. It wanted Ajit to come back! Ajit could be seen strolling alone in the garden, scavenging for unknown things and sitting in the veranda for time-lost hours. He would watch the stopped clocks of the half-buried rooms like a never-ending dream. He would gape at the old courtyard for eternity. Sometimes, he walked around smelling the dead candle wax in ancient sconces mounted on the black walls of a hopeless dwelling! Many days, he hurried back from the office and sat on his bed, doing nothing but feeling good – feeling really very good! The house would comfort him; he did not feel like going anywhere else. He stopped going to the factory. He just wanted to spend as much time as possible in the landlord's house – No! His palace! His Palace with red and yellow glass panes, wrapped in cobweb and dust, the dream of castle lanterns! Dipped in fantasy and between the new, fresh wind of cackling secrets, a second life started in the tenant.

A month went by like this, and still, there was no sign of the landlord's return. Ajit was happy, he lived in the castle alone, looking out of its oriel windows at the world - the sea of brown roofs, the many uninhabited houses and the abandoned forests covered in the evening fog as if everything was his! His dark forbidden empire! The thought maddened him with an unrestrained joyousness. Ajit was not very fond of drinking, but the urge to consume liquor got him lately. So, he asked Rohini to complete her chores as soon as possible and leave early so that he can drink, so that he can listen to the valleys of sinister flowers sing to him every night! Sing as the gossamer lanterns of old forgotten palace rocks on the walls of winter dark!

'Sir, is everything okay?' asked Rohini one evening, while making snacks. 'You look tired, should I get you anything? Sir'

"Everything is fine, Rohini", responded Ajit calmly, savouring the snacks with a sauce made from a local hillside herb. He then quickly retired to his room, silently closing the door behind.

It is the third week of December, and the forests behind the century-old palace lie covered in a grimy darkness. The seventy-year-old landlord had finally returned from his brother's house. He was feeling less morose between the dead walls of his grim house. Ajit remained closed behind his door, sometimes drinking liquor, sometimes listening to the harrowing songs on the old radio. Ajit showed no signs of leaving the room. Worried, the fatherly landlord asked Rohini about Ajit.

"Ajit Babu has changed, he eats meat every day, he can't live with alcohol,' has informed the faithful maid. Also, Rohini told him how Ajit kept roaming in the palace listlessly, staring into the void – gaping at the starless night. Rohini expressed how afraid she was while coming into the house, and many times, while leaving the house at night, she has heard some cackles coming from the basement - the basement which the landlord has shut down for ages! The seventy-year-old landlord fell into a deep thought, and the wrinkles around his furrowed eyes grew deeper.

Lying in his armchair, he leaned his head forward. He asked Rohini quietly, "He has not gone anywhere near the basement, has he, Rohini? Or have you?!"

"No, Dadaji" replied the frightened girl, confirming.

An owl sat on the last branch of the lonely garden tree, a bland moon coming out!

"Your mother has spent thirty years in this place, Rohini, she knows what I am telling", said the old man, his hands trembling. He stared at the yellow lantern lit in the vast, empty hallway and went on "Your mother knows the tale. She must have told you!?"

"Yes", answers Rohini as shortly as she could, her throat drying up.

"Nobody goes near that basement. Nobody has, in the last hundred years!" pressed the old lips of the landlord, sensing an ominous danger. "You must ignore what you hear, Rohini. You must stay away from there!"

"Yes… Yes Dadaji," stammers Rohini, looking in the same direction as the evening lantern where the senile man was gawking at.

“I don’t think Ajit Babu knows there is a basement in this house; none of us has told him about it. But I wonder if he has found it!” stated Rohini, more scared than ever.

“No, no, he must not!” The old landlord sank back in his chair, a fright catching his little grey eyebrows.

Rohini looked equally pensive, a fatigue made of particles of fear caught her pale blue eyes. A fragile blow of faint wind winkingly streamed across the meadows, the windows, and finally, gushed past their evening lantern, floating down to the dark of the basement. Rohini and the old landlord, both saw it! There lived a mystery, locked behind the carcass doors!

A pair of steps could be heard from the side of the courtyard, a shadow walking in moonlight towards the submerged night that remained beneath winding stairs.

‘Must be Ajit. I need to talk to him,’ said the old man.

“I will inform Sir,” assured Rohini.

“But tell him that I have invited him over for dinner tonight,” said the old landlord, taking quick measures.

Rohini shook her head and rambled towards the black moonlit courtyard, her saree cutting through hush hush sounds of the sad night wind!

It was five past ten of a lonely, cold night, and the valley of the neighbourhood slept in a morose silence. Rohini finished her cooking and left for the day. The loadshedding has taken out all the lights - the iron-rimmed fog-fed staircases wound down into a sinister mystery of the uncanny past. The courtyard, its cobbled stones lay dead in the dead of a lifeless night. Sometimes, what people think, sometimes the tales that people search for are the tales that search for them, life for life, death for death and Ajit wanted to live the tale – he was living it now! The tale of desire! He must get what he has desired - this palace, its blankness with all its black glass-panes was his now! The glow of amber light coming from the wrinkled man's room fell on the hoarse cobbled stones, revealing the obscure path to Ajit, who strolled now drunken but steady, towards the destiny that lures, unravelling!

Knocking, the tenant stood outside the damped door and a shaky but still holding firm - a voice of a wrinkled old man reverberated from inside, "Come in, Ajit."

Ajit entered, staring at the unclean fire shelf, the criss-crosses of spiderwebs around the rusted almirah. He sat down on a skeletal chair facing the threadbare, candle-lit table on which sat glimmering dishes of two different kinds of fish, a large bowl of curry, and lumps of rice.

The old landlord fetched Ajit some rice and curry and, with slender, wrinkled hands, fetched the rest on his own hot plate. Five minutes passed, and they ate in silence, the candle fluttering soundlessly in hot air of the cold night.

"How is your work going, Ajit?" asked the landlord in a fatherly, tender tone.

"Fine, it is going fine", replied the tenant, his eyes down.

"Okay," said the landlord." What did you do here when I was out of station? Hope you did not have any problem here, Ajit?" enquired the wrinkled old man, in a sombre tone.

A gust of the wind, spreading its wings, weaved through the old mortar palace. The wind formless appeared on the obscure charcoal walls - the shadow of the branches of a leaky, deaf tree that stood lanky, leaning towards the spectre of the cursed, desolate fortress.

"I managed," replied Ajit, making no eye contact.

Another ten minutes went by in silence while the old man, between his eating, stopped and watched Ajit closely. Yes, Ajit looks aged and unkept now; his demeanour has changed from a young, promising man to that of a tired, careless, more aged person. In the burning yellow of the hot candle, the old, wrinkled landlord placed his little grey eyes on the deceased, dead skin of hanging animals which lay still, frozen in time of a dark past. A deer, the face of a vulture watched them from the high palace walls.

"Ajit, I will ask you something, which you might find a bit odd, but I must ask you. Please do answer truthfully," demanded the old man, in the way of a father who was trying to protect his son.

'Yes,' replied Ajit, without looking up.

'Have you heard anything strange in this house?' asked the old man.

'No' said Ajit promptly, his heart pounding.

Disappointed knowing Ajit is not telling the truth, he enquired again, "Have you ever been near the basement, Ajit?"

Ajit stopped eating and, in the burning yellow of the candle flame, fixing his fearful eyes on the old man, angrily he said 'No, I have not been".

A pulse of heightening fear and anxiety ran through the old man's veins as he shadowed the excitement of a young yet aged Ajit.

"You look tired. Have some water", said Ajit, in a gruelling tone and passed the heavy copper glass.

The shadow of Ajit cast in the candlelight now looked much bigger and fiendish!

Afraid, the rumpled, trembling old landlord pleaded, "Do not go there, Ajit. Ever!"

Finishing the dinner, Ajit silently walked out of the old man's eroded room. The wind, the gust, the stream of a misty, mysterious, dead night played like a child's cackle in the air of desolate palace rooms. The candle has been extinguished now! Ajit has been clever! He has done what was needed – the old landlord, now lay, blue and frothed out, with his head bent down on the table - dead! How quick and how finely cruel he has been! But no, this house, this vast, vacant mystic palace belongs to him, only to him, he is the King! The only landlord here!!

Ajit had planned this night for weeks, when he had all the time in the world while living alone in this house. He has felt that the house, the mystery and past, the broken soul of the bleak palace, needed him. Walking proudly by its veranda and fiendish staircases, he felt lately that something which entered this house a long time ago has still not left, something that is reaching out to him, something that infuses his soul with vigour - a power that he relishes! From antique showpieces to the wool-gathering courtyard, from the wildflowers invoking magic on broken wings of flying moths to the hanging old torches by the wells - he owns everything. There might be something more precious hidden in the basement, Ajit knows it! Although the old man did not want him to know about the secret, the thing that lives on, the strange cackle which he heard, had let him know everything. "He must protect the house, the tale it embodies!' The cackles and the voices have never talked to him directly but have shown him in mysterious ways what needs to be done.

Tonight, he has committed the act as it was meant to be! While the old man ate his food looking downwards, he had quickly put the poison in the glass of water and even quicker, the wrinkled face of the old hag had turned pale and distorted! Then, taking the keys from the dead man's pocket, he has left the old landlord behind to rot there, to rot there alone. Now, he can have all the gems and jewels that lay hidden in the forbidden basement!

Without wasting any moment, Ajit darted towards the basement. He walked down the razor-sharp edges of the mottled staircase, spellbound in the dark of a wintry night. Strangely though, within all this moonless darkness, he knew where he is heading to - some unearthly voices directly murmured to his ears now! Under the call of a roguish spell, he unlocked the rotten cold lock of the basement and then, in the thrill of jewels, he walked past the bony dungeons which slept hidden in the forever dark of ages. Drowsy, he now walked towards a faint gleam of an intriguing will-o'-wisp which kept coming from the far corner of the hidden palace basement!

Ajit, sleepy, moseyed slowly through the airless silence of marshy walls, and finally, he got to the source of the bizarre gleam! An altar, he discovered - an altar with some dry flowers and two burning black candles.

'Who lights the candles?? Who comes in the basement?!' thinking, he gasped for air and by the black candlelight, he discovered one more thing – his ajar eyes stuck in wonder! - a jewel-studded casket! Curious and breathing in the black breeze of a mystic night, raised by hopes and hairs of burning blackening fantasies, Ajit felt like he had travelled back in time, swooned past centuries to find the castle's cursed treasure! His nomadic gaze flickered in the rhombus gleam of black candles! Mad he felt! The power he held! His hands quivered as he picked the gleaming casket, mystical zephyrs and rubies laid on it like offerings of some mythical occult rituals! The more he touched the rubies, the black candles flickered even more! Ajit was filled with a speechless gratitude towards whoever had guided him to this place!

Some moments of Ajit holding the strange ancient casket passed - his eyes beaming with triumph! All his sins will be forgotten. *He is a King now*! Suddenly, the gaunt pillars of the underground cellar shook! An icy cold gust of unsound black reaved the altar, one candle fell dead! The other candle fought fading but still holding one last flush of a dying soul – in whose little light unlocked five rotten secret doors hidden in-the-wall! Ajit watched in terror! Five round white faces with sad, blood-soaked eyes came out! What are those?! A terrible terror curdled into his spine as the pale white faces with blood dripping eyes floated into the shivering black of lamp-less dungeon!!

Seeing what he did not want to see – *five white faces with razor-sharp teeth floating out from the blue cellar and coming towards him*! Ajit fell on the ground, scared witless, muttering something! The casket fell, dousing the last black candle – the besieged white hair of heinous creatures flying terribly in the blue-black midair!

The doomed man saw their long nails meandering towards him – a call of sinful ages, a coveting of centuries! They have waited a hundred years, hidden in the basement! They have waited and waited and now has come the *night of the tale*! The curse has lived – a dozen long white nails tore through Ajit's flesh and bone. His head fell dead pale on the moth-eaten cellar floor, his greedy eyes ajar, petrified with fear!

MISHA'S DOLLS

Misha's grandmother made seven dolls for Misha - all woven in wool, spiralled beautifully through tapestry needles. Misha had each of them scheduled for play - red for Monday, yellow for Wednesday, blue for Tuesday and violet for Thursday. The pretty green doll walked out of the closet on Friday! The black and the white dolls were weekend special!!

August, September and October went by in the same fashion, and then suddenly the *doll order* was broken! Misha would choose one randomly and play with it. Nevertheless, she was happy. The winter rushed through the windows- the crisp snow started to fall!

In blue-white mornings of curling sprinkling snow, Misha played- engrossed with her dolls!! The school closed for winter vacation, and she had nothing much to do. Her mother made warm, pleasant foods in the kitchen, her father was away to an unknown town for work. Misha's world revolved around her seven woollen dolls.

"May I come in?" said a woman's voice from the door.

"Must be our tailor's daughter Rita. She has come to return the shirts," said Misha's mother, hurrying to the door.

To her surprise, instead of Rita, stood a middle-aged woman in a long black gown. Her hair tied neatly in a bun- she had a smile on her face. Misha's mother was surprised. Surely what she heard was Rita's voice, but no, she was wrong! Stranger even, the lady's left arm was bandaged up to her little finger.

"How can I help you?" asked Misha's mother in a serious tone.

"Nothing, if you had something to stop this," said the lady, extending her right index finger. There was a small red cut in its tip. "It is hurting!" said she, holding the strange flat smile.

Misha's mother looked up at the medicine shop across the street but found it to be closed. She then looked at the hospital at the end of the lane- the psychiatric hospital.

"You might- might get help there!" stuttered Misha's mother, showing her the hospital.

"Just a small thing, they won't attend me there," replied the stranger in a calm voice.

"Sure,' said Misha's mother hesitantly and let her in.

The stranger followed her to the kitchen but stood outside. Misha's mother said something to Misha's grandmother in a low voice - nothing could be heard! Misha's grandmother soon came out holding a silver tray in hand. It had a cotton ball, an antiseptic and a small piece of roller bandage. Misha's grandma first pressed the stranger's finger with the cotton ball and held it tightly for a while. Once the blood clotted, she cleaned the area with the antiseptic, which she carefully procured from the bottle. Then, gently holding the edge of her finger, the old lady put another small cotton pad over the cut and bandaged the finger. When she left the stranger's hand, she found her watching Misha playing with dolls.

"What a lovely child!" said she, looking at the confused old grandma. "My name is Mary Anne. I came here to visit the church.'

"Okay!" said the charming old grandma, still looking at her bandaged arm with great curiosity.

"I brushed my finger against a little thorn and got this silly thing! Thank you for your help."

"No problem!" said the old lady.

The stranger left. Both Misha's mother and grandmother watched her leave. Misha too.

At night, Misha sleepily crawled up to her mushy bed and fell asleep. She, after all, had a tiring, long day of doll play! It was only two hours later when she woke up, and she was perspiring hard! Through her window may be or may be through a thin film of a ghastly dream - she has seen a woman, the same woman of the morning! She was dressed in black! In her dreams, she has seen her standing below their stairs - the same place where Grandma dressed her cut. One thing, though, her eyes were different. Her eyes, like her clothes, were jet black! Misha started trembling again- the dream was strange, ominous and foreboding! She saw the peculiar woman extending her slender, bandaged hand towards the stairs and chortling!! His hands (Misha remembered *dreading*) were long, growing, so sinister inhumane! But her eyes- that woman's eyes dilated, pitch-black!

Misha sprang up on her bed - she remembered the name suddenly - Mary Anne! A chill ran down her spine! Her mother was sleeping beside her. She looked at her face, she was asleep- really deep asleep! Misha, terrified by the nightmare, heard something now – a faint dragging of footsteps up the stairs! Up-and-loose the feet came, one step, two step closer! Misha was terrorised. She felt dizzy- mortified with fear!!

"Is it grandma?" she thought, and in that very moment, a loud thud struck their bedroom door! It was a cruel thud- a deafening thud! The door banged open with the stranger lady's bandaged hand entering first

- then her morbid face with those grotesque black eyes, her red teeth hanging from her broken lips! Misha shook her mother violently, who slept spellbound in a deep, tranquil. Frightened to protect herself, Misha jumped down quickly from the bed and opened the back door, almost tumbling downstairs to the petrifying dark! The wraith floating in the air followed her from behind as she rolled down, crumbling with terror to the lightless corridor!!

On hitting the floor, she bled badly, but the fear of death is far more fearful than the fear of blood. Misha ran to her grandma. She, too, like her mother, has been mounted to a death spell sleep. Even after violent shaking and endless pleading, she did not show any sign of movement!

Helpless, Misha aimed for the main door but fell on her knees, hurting herself gravely. She felt an excruciating pain, but crawled! Crawling on her knees, bleeding, she looked back again - the pair of horrendous hands with long nails still coming at her, but seeing something, it stopped! The witch with ghastly enlarged black eyes stopped moving! Misha is bleeding heavily now, stopped crawling! On windows and shelves, she found six of her dolls standing - all faced in the occultist's way! The sorceress tried fiercely, but she could not move as if something fierce was overpowering her- her long hands and legs were being forced reverse! A cruel, terrible sight it was!! Misha, frozen in shock, saw something. In front of a distorting Mary Anne, was something – it was her seventh doll! The Black Rag Doll!!

THE TULIP STEALER

A man jumped off a tree, crossed the fence and entered the garden. The garden had big and little flowers - some daisies, many sunflowers, mixed roses and a lot of tulips. Lovely pink tulips grew in a cross maze of flowery bed- a few wasps encircled them! A man in unkempt clothes, keeping his head down, walked quickly into the tall grasses. He must stay there, hidden from the garden owner, Mr Bansal.

Mr Bansal was an eighty-three-year-old man. Although aged, he was still as sharp as a tiger - a little sound here and there, and there you go, he is awake! This is what the man hidden in grasses was worried about. If he gets caught this time, he will go straight to prison!

The man waited twenty-eight minutes and thirty-something seconds between the blades of tall grass - mosquitoes and ants biting him all over!! With such pain and sweats, he was still onto the job he had come for- "Oh, those splendid tulips! They will put some money in my pocket," his face brightened up with the thought. The sunflowers smiled brighter in the yellow daylight!

With no sign of Mr Bansal around, he stood up from the prickly grasses and peeped into the house through a glass-pane. There was nobody in there!

"Must be sleeping in his room- the Old Hag!" thought the crook smiling- silently (and stealthily!) making his way towards the priceless tulips. The lean legs of the flower thief sprang up and down like hollow *stilts* as there were springs fitted under her feet!

"One, two, three, four... five, six, seven", he crooned, choosing the tulips with his artful finger. Then, quickly putting his sly fingers down the pocket, he took out a pair of silver scissors. The scissors were 'bent' like him and have helped him in many of his crooked endeavours. With fast hands and seven clicks, he had what he wanted - the Seven Pink Tulips of the most exquisite strain!

Taking the same cobbled path back, he went out of the garden. A sigh of relief!

At some time, he was in the market, standing near the florist.

"What have you bought today?" asked the fat florist, spraying his roadside flower display.

The flower thief- the vagabond- *the tulip stealer* hastily produced what he had just procured from Mr Bansal's Garden. The florist looked surprised- somewhat annoyed. Seeing what he was holding in his own hands, a terror coursed through his veins! In place of seven fresh tulips, in his hands were seven dead, decayed, perished tulips!

THE BURNT POT

This story is not bred from my imagination or a sick poem of a forgotten time- it is a stone-hard reality of some family having gone through it. It was told to me by somebody I met in the Missionaries of Charity. He was on a world tour, made a Korean friend who originally told him this story. I came in the string of people who were destined to hear this breaking tale – this fierce tale is of a Korean family. A tale of sheer pain veering through agony where nothing remains of it - this whatever it is-was speaks of that! I have tried to make the story a little odd, funny to absorb from it- tearing colours of dread, but I failed...

Hopi and Jopi were playing since morning. Their mothers kept talking in the kitchen. Hopi and Jopi were frolicking from here to there – one picking stones, the other picking dirt, playing hide-and-seek, throwing flying disks! The mothers made no fuss of the ruckus. They were used to it.

The mishap happened when they started running tirelessly through the rooms, despite their mothers shouting, "Hopi, Jopi, do not run so much!"

What happened exactly was that both Hopi and Jopi ran to seize the earthen pot lying in the garden. It was a burnt earth pot- mottled from all sides, hays and straw came out of its open mouth. The two silly billies ran in from opposite sides, colliding, falling together on the pot- breaking it into pieces! As soon as it broke, something black spilt out, roiling the ground.

Their mothers talked, laughed and jibber-jabbered the whole afternoon. They never heard anything. When they came searching for their lads in the dead of the evening, there was a hideous thing standing in the black garden. It had half the face of Hopi, half the face of Jopi – the two faces somewhat crudely stitched from the middle! The black stitch dangled down in cruel air, ending in a skinning needle! Their faces have been sutured forcefully. It was most harrowing to look at, painful too!! Both their mothers fainted at the horrid sight.

A CASE OF LIONOLIA

Dishu could not remember anything. Beatings, scoldings, chocolate bribing - all done, but Dishu could not remember his lessons. Dishu's mother made good food for him. Dishu's father ran to priests and physicians to help his eight-year-old son memorise school lessons, but nobody could help Dishu. Soon, everybody had to accept it as a curse of destiny.

After finding one thousand and one hundred solutions that could not solve his son's problem, Dishant's father went to see the new doctor sitting in the local dispensary. A very learned man, everybody has said. He can cure everything, everybody has assured.

When Dishu's father entered the consultation chamber, he saw a middle-aged man with a large moustache and fat belly, smiling at him. He had a habit- a predisposition worse- to bite his nails every few seconds. The smoke in the chamber also suggested he had an addiction. The man did not seem right in his head!

"A clear case of gastritis due to hiatal hernia. How is the pain now? Are you nauseated?" rambled the physician, the scar across his left eyebrow bent down and up.

"Sorry?!" said the boy's father, confusedly. "Oh! No! No! I have come here for my son. He cannot memorise anything."

A boy in a red cap hurried into the chamber and sat on a chair.

The learned man with a boil on his face took up his stethoscope to begin with the examination. After checking Dishu's eyes, ears, tongue, lungs, chest and belly for the next few minutes, the nervous doctor returned to his chair. He was shaking and talking to himself- a complete lunatic!

"Ok! Okay! Which standard are you in Dishu?" asked the strange doctor, with the most exciting curiosity, the thrill thrilling- spurring the sense of the child.

The boy with a round face, round eyes, and round spectacles said nothing.

"Ok! Okay! Can you tell me what 12 plus 7 is?" asked the crack-brained doctor again.

Dishu remained silent. He stared blankly at the interrogator's face. His oddly still eyes did not even blink.

"Ok! Okay! Can you name an animal whose colour is grey?" asked this ridiculous question, the nutcase doctor, waiting patiently. Dishu sat there wordless, lip tight, looking sillily at the silly doctor. "What child does not know an elephant? He is truly a fool, a complete nitwit, a head-zero cow!" thought the hopeless father, rapidly losing hope in a surge of growing anxiety. He was just about to lash out at his *cursed* son when the unusual interrogator spoke again, "Alright! How many friends do you have?"

"Five - Jatin, Tilu, Heena, Romi, Priya," replied Dishu, suddenly breaking the spell of silence.

"Ok! Okay! A clear case of Lionolia," inferred the hare-brained physician, the boil showing bigger with the dilating smile.

"Is it very serious?" asked the father, eyebrows raised, his face bloodless with fear.

"Oh! No! No at all. Just some nerves in the little brain not working," he bit his nails and continued, "Precisely two nerves. A bit of Lionolia will get them going," replied the crackhead fella. He quickly took out his pad and scribbled down everything in a handwriting most obscure to mankind. Then he offered the writing, more peculiar than a papyrus of lost ages, to the fool's father. The mad doctor, instead of writing much, has drawn a strange child face with two whip ropes coming out of its head – maybe the *two erred nerves* he was stressed about! Adjacent to the eerie drawing was a bottle drawn with the most devious slants. At the chest of the bottle was written "LION-OLIA."

Dishant's father took his eyes off the occult paper, his skull sockets paining with disbelief! He looked up at the strange man who was smiling crookedly again- his brow mark bending towards the dead houseplant. "Where has he come? For what sin was he being punished like this?" That's all he could think. Hesitantly and sunk in deep melancholy, he bought the big tonic bottle labelled as LION-OLIA from the pharmacy.

Dishu was given the tonic, three teaspoons every night before going to bed. In a week, the changes were seen - Dishant was doing his chores really fast, his memory sharpened, his interest in studies grew. He additionally helped his mother sort the red and green vegetables, naming them one by one like a parrot.

When his father returned from work, Dishu would tell him about the planets, their colours, the sun and the moon. He even warned everybody of the harmful plants and insects that should not be touched at any cost. More than astonishment, everyone in the family was thrilled - Dishu could remember his studies, the curse was finally lifted!

Dishu's mother, father, aunt and uncle - everybody went to thank the mad doctor.

"I am glad he is cured," said the mad doctor humbly.

Curious, Dishu's aunt took out the Lionolia bottle and asked, "What is this magic medicine! We have not heard of it before."

"Oh! That thing," said the lunatic, snatching the magic tonic from her hand. Then, suddenly opening its cap, he started drinking from it - the remaining medicine!

"What! Have you gone mad?!" echoed everyone together, baffled.

"Oh! This is nothing. Just some oil made from dead lions," assured the loon.

THE SILENT TOWN

This story was told to me by a school friend's father. It may have happened with a friend of his who was also a photographer.

Being a nature photographer, Nirav's job was to take the best pictures from different parts of the country. Nirav loved rivers and birds. He liked the chirping of insects, the babbling of streams. He was also a fast learner of things. Once, during his stay near a tea garden, he learned all about the tea leaves- their way of harvesting, their flavours and every other thing. Nirav liked exploring new places, sitting under the trees, talking to locals and in this little way of merry making, his life passed cheerfully. Always very decent, kind and amiable, he never said no to any work, he did them all with an open heart. Rain or winter, he walked the rifts and cliffs, searching for nests and trails, timber and rails.

"How exquisite?" said Nirav's manager often. "Your pictures reek of Mother Nature. There is a story in every leaf! "

"Thank you, sir, I am always trying," has replied Nirav, always.

One evening, Nirav was sitting in a village shed enjoying the rain. Suddenly, his phone rang. Hurriedly, he picked up the call. It was his manager.

"Hello, Nirav! You have to visit Maithipur for some days."

"Maithipur? Where exactly is it, Bishambar sir?"

"South Himachal. It is a hill town, a beautiful place really," replied the manager.

"But I have never been to Himachal ever. I don't know anything there. Can you find me a different..."

"No! No! Maithipur is a little nice town," shot the manager, not letting Nirav complete. "You are leaving first thing in the morning!" The call got disconnected.

The dripping evening rain that looked riveting a moment before changed to slow, heavy droplets of a hard, uncertain life.

The next day, Nirav boarded the train on time. It was a seventeen-hour journey. Nirav took pictures of the landscape through the train's window. Then, he fell asleep. He lost count of time until a thundering jerk woke him up in the middle of the night. The train stopped abruptly! It was also in the same moment that Nirav realised he had reached his destination, Maithipur.

As soon as he down from the train, a man with a lantern approached him.

"Are you Nirav Babu?" asked the man in a very kind voice.

'Yes,' replied the tourist.

"I am Bishnu. I will take you to the hotel."

Quickly, Bishnu lit the lantern and soon, in a cold winter night of whooshing, the two were seen walking, trailed by their own shadows!

After nearly twenty minutes of walking, Nirav reached the appointed lodging. It did not look like a hotel at all. It was a one-storey house with hardly three rooms. Bishnu helped Nirav with some food and left for the day. Nirav, who was very tired, fell asleep fast.

The next morning, Nirav woke up, got ready and went out for a walk. The place looked abandoned- most barren. First, he came across a left settlement with empty huts and empty cow sheds. Then he came across a well with no water. He then found a hive with no bees, followed by a stable with no horses. All his strange curiosity came to an end when he saw some people working at a near distance. Taking a few more steps towards them, he found out it was a town.

It was a strange little town where everybody worked in silence. The horsemen fed the grasses, the tailor stitched clothes, the apothecaries kept medicines, the blacksmiths welded iron - only the sound of machines and things, not a single person talked! Nirav watched everything with incredible wonder, he even tried to communicate with a lady who sold spun wool.

"Hello, how much is that wool?" asked Nirav, pointing towards a brown wool ball.

The woman answered Nirav by showing him the price chart. Simple and easy!

Nirav then came to a point from where the town's main road started - the midday sun fell on the paths clad with snow. It was cold, people wore blue-green sweaters, the children were smiling, but all were very silent. Shops after shops, homes after homes passed by – Nirav saw nobody talking, just some hand signs, and they were good! Life went on.

Soon, Nirav reached the flower shop, which stood at the end of the small town. The shop caught Nirav's attention from a distance. It had amazing flowers - yellow, pink, orange-violet flowers with such large petals! Nirav has never seen flowers with such big petals before! He was naturally attracted to them.

Walking nearer, he started photographing them from different angles. The flower seller with freckles on one side of his face said nothing. Nirav enjoyed the silence written in every corner of the snowing hill town – he kept taking the flower photographs.

After he was done, he asked the flower seller, "What's the prettiest flower you have got?"

The silent florist, maintaining the silent rule of the town, raised his index finger towards a specific flower pot. It was hidden behind a bunch of other flowers. Taking a few steps back, Nirav finally saw those pastel green flowers with utter bedazzlement. The large green petals shimmered in the clattering sunlight. Their stalks were coiled in spirals. He fell short of words! He became as speechless as the people of Maithipur.

"Where did you get these flowers?" asked Nirav, quickly gazing at the possibility of photographing an entire field of such exotic, mesmerising flowers. "Wouldn't it be great?" thought Nirav.

The flower seller pointed his finger towards a place which was up in the mountains.

"Thank you," said Nirav, and got going.

After a painstaking journey through curving paths, thorns, spruce and firs, Nirav reached a forest. The forest was sprinkled with snow and had only kind of flowers – the same strange green flowers bloomed everywhere! Again, the same smell- the same call of phantasmagoria! Nirav just stood there – revering their beauty!

Ambling towards the sea of green flowers as if drawn towards them, he started feeling sleepy. Nirav could not stop; his feet walked on their own. Reaching near, he found that the trees that produced these joyous green flowers had a very thick bark. The bark secreted a resin which was also green. He strolled between the ocean of green flowers for a while and then took out his camera. He adjusted its lens and, in a sleepy, drowsy air of green everything, Nirav started capturing the unreal paradise!

Hours and sand of the dunes passed by, Nirav lost count of time. His spell was broken when a strong cold wind reeked his eyes and ears. The winds started picking up, and Nirav ran in pursuit of a secure shade. In the blink of an eye, the wind changed to a snowy storm- the trees started to shake and break. His sight blocked by falling arrows of snow blades forced to turn by a crevasse. He slipped but ran. Some blades struck Nirav; he panged with pain. Nirav ran as fast as he could, and sliding down a block of ice, he reached a wall. The wall looked like a remnant of an ancient temple; what remained of it was just the wall with some wrecked ceiling. Exhausted with insufferable pain, Nirav sat down by the hedge - hail and snow darting in through the wall holes! Time passed, but the storm showed no sign of stopping. His legs and hands bled badly. He shouted for help but in vain. Some moments later, out of a sad rending pain, Nirav lost consciousness.

Deep in the night, Nirav woke up. The storm has stopped, but he feels a terrible pain in his whole body. His heart was pounding, and his chest felt heavy. He also had a high fever and could not move his legs. Everything from his camera to his watch to his phone was broken. He dozed off again.

Two days or so, he lay in one position, fractured, his senses coming and going. Sometimes, through the corner of his half-closed eyes, he saw the green flowers of the forest – sometimes he just stared at the snow. 'Hunger, thirst and loneliness have left him on the door of death,' he understood that. The night fell over, and the cold wind started to blow again. He opened his feverish eyes one last time and thought of the good memories lived – the forests, the rivers, the towns, his father, mother, sister! The wind grew harder - the hailstones started to fall on the walls. He closed his eyes.

Deep night in winter black, the dying man heard a humming sound, someone was walking behind the walls singing – a woman! With foggy eyes, he saw a lady in a black cloak putting a *green something* in the wall-holes. She quickly walked to him – a bowl of *glowing, fuming green* held in her long, bony hands. She looked old from the way her grey hair spread out, flying towards the hoary moon. With her face hidden behind the cloak, she touched Nirav. Her touch made him sleepier! From the flowy bowl, she put the vicious green all over his wounds, his forehead. It reminded him of the green flowers, the resins that dripped from them! Anxious, he tried to see her, but a hazy cloak of fleeting snow flew amidst. She kept pouring the fuming green into his blood pores, his racking gores. She, from her sinistrous black hide, put the *Ator* in his broken joints, passing through an infernal *rack* - a mound of hellion curse romped in his veins! He wanted to shriek, but the nefarious coffin digger put the Ator in his lips – he struggled for breath! Then, in a blinding rain of hoarfrost, in a dark rime of hiding rots, he saw her in the blackest night! She- who carried *bleeding green eyes*!! There is an art of putting an end to things, she, the bone eater- the walker of graves, knew it. Nirav felt a hurting opening in his ribs, his bones cracking – his chest bones arching in his last breath. Dying, the night falling into more night!

AUNT CLAIRE

Brian came back home after ten long months. He has completed his high school and will be going to college very soon. All this house-shifting drama was unsettling him, so he went straight to his parents, especially to his father, telling him, “I need to chill a few days before going to college. I had too much on me in the last few months. The studies, the exams – oh, the books!”

“Brian, if you will not work hard at this age. Then when will you?” asked his father in a characteristic cold tone.

Brian did not bother to reply. He made a bored face and looked outside the window.

“Your father is right, Brian. You have only a month to rest. Rest as much as you want, but then start preparing for your college,” said Brian’s mother in the most cold-hearted way.

Brian, uninterested in the conversation, did not answer.

The next day, Brian’s parents took a plane to San Francisco. His father was a rich businessman. So, he always had to be conscious of the trade so that he would not turn poor anytime soon. Brian’s mother was a shadow to his father. She never went against any of his words. She went wherever her husband went.

Brian had nothing much to do. He mostly slept all day, watched television and then went back to sleep.

One day, he called up some of his friends. He asked them to come over, but they refused, saying the travelling distance would not make up for the time. Brian returned to watching television and then playing his stupid video games again. After accomplishing all trivial missions with much pretence, he came back to the mobile phone again. It showed One Missed Call! Aunt Claire!

A sudden glow came to Brian's face. There he was, smiling, thinking of her – Aunt Claire. She was his father's sister, his only sister. She lives in New Orleans now – cannot walk much - was old - had two servants- this was the information obtained when he last talked to Aunt Claire. Brain happy and smiling, ringed back Aunty Claire.

Ring, Ring! The phone rang! Somebody picked up.

"Hello, Aunty Claire! This is Brian."

"Do I sound like your aunt, boy?" said a man in a rude voice.

"No! But!" Brian fell short of words- he was taken aback. "Can you give the phone to Aunt Claire,' Brain insisted, keeping his calm.

"There ain't no Claire here," said the uninterested man again.

"Wrong number!?" he thought. As his thoughts blobbed and pushed through hard, the phone got disconnected!

Brian checked the number he had just dialled. It was of a different person! His face paled. He searched the call log for Aunt Claire's number but could not find it.

The outside dark of the falling night greyed out the nature, the evening mysterious and deeply reminiscent of an old Aunt Claire came, came back. "How could he make such a mistake? He has her missed call!"

A hellbent shock – a tingling ran down his spine instantly when he saw his dead aunt's portrait in the drawing room, "Isn't she dead already two months?!"

SNDHUK'S PARCEL

The deliveryman ran up the stairs and reached the second floor. There were only two flats on the floor. He first checked the left flat's number, then the right's and then the name written on the parcel, along with the address written. The delivery man held the parcel tight and walked straight towards the flat on the right. The door was quite old, like the other doors.

"Maybe an old establishment, maybe old residents who have been living for a long time," thought the man.

Without wasting any time, he pressed the doorbell, which rang quite spiritually with the sounds of Gods. He waited, but nobody came. Getting late, he pensively pressed the bell again. This time, a faint hint of steps was heard from inside. Somebody approached the door and then, turning the knob from inside, she opened the door. It was one old, worn-out house that suddenly popped in front of his eyes. The cobwebs and the very old walls gaped from inside, the air aged, dusty and forgotten. Standing in front of him was an old woman, her big eyes hid behind heavy glasses.

"Sandhuk Lodha?" asked the deliveryman.

"Oh! Oh!" said the woman in feeblest of voices. The man waited for her to complete. The old grandma purred, "Oh! He is my husband. He has gone outside. Come back tomorrow," saying she hurried to close the door.

"Madam, you can receive it too, you just have to sign, can you do that?"

The old lady looked in and out, then right and left, thinking something, her fingers old and wrinkled, often trembled. "Oh! Sure" she replied, her eyes were kind.

She took the pen and signed feebly on the row shown by the man. The delivery man gave her the parcel. Taking, she went inside.

Coming a flight of stairs down, he remembered something. He quickly checked the other parcel in his hand - it had the name of Sandhuk Lodha! Quickly inferring his mistake, he ran up the stairs he had just come down and went back to the flat. He knocked on the door and was about to ring the bell when the door opened suddenly – no creaking at all, just the door opened ajar! He was about to call out when he saw something, and his hands stiffened up to his neck, chilling his bones with a cold wire. Through the parallel walls of the broken, moth-eaten green walls, when his eyes fell on the last room rendered tiny by farness, there was Mrs. Lodha walking on the walls, latching onto the ceiling, hanging down from cobwebs! Her long, leaky hands almost reached the opposite wall where sparrows cried trapped in cross webs!! She picked them one by one and ate mercilessly!

FORBIDDING

One of my students told me this story. This is a very sad story that left a deep scar on me. I am unsure of how much truth exists, for I will be relieved if there is none, but the mind can't forget the darkness, the pain in the eyes (the pain caused- suffered by the eyes)- the severe trepidation I felt! I, in my most cruel dreams, cruel self- will not- will never wish it upon someone!

I've heard a lot of stories. I know many stories, but this one is little different. It will be wrong to call it a story; it's a fact- a real occurrence. Whether the story is true or not, it opens a door to a new world- a strange realm – a place where nothing- nothing good happens! An abode where there is only death and demolition.

This story- the most unique and terrifying- rending- causes me a pain most terrible, a sadness most destructive! This tale (the abysmal, uncanny and terrible) that hinges- opens- breaks the door to a terrifying reality, leaves in me- no humane sanctity whatsoever left! Whatever it is, I am torn to shreds, a despair most never-ending and mutilating has harrowed me! I will never be the same again.

The incident happened with a patient admitted in hospital. I can't name the patient or the hospital, otherwise it will cause terror. People wouldn't want to go there. The patient was a woman. This woman was hospitalised in this institution for quite some time. She spent day after day in the forsaken place, but her condition did not improve. Medicines were prescribed, doctors came, but she, the sick laid restless on a sick bed, drained and ruined! The long-standing illness bound her to bed for weeks and months. Her body became weak, her mind weaker. Her family came to see her almost every day, but the terrible affliction never left her.

One night when the rest of the patients were sleeping, she got out of her bed and went to the hospital bathroom. There she saw another woman sitting in front of a bucket, taking a bath. She faced the wall. Even after several attempts, she couldn't see her face. This woman kept on taking a bath facing the wall, she tried and tried but could not see her. She kept bathing in the middle of the night.

And then something might have happened! Maybe the woman who was showering has turned her face and looked at her (it is still unknown). But the patient caught a fever- a strange, high fever from that night! The doctors and nurses tried their best, but the fever did not subside. Although she came from a poor household, she was served by a lot of love and care. Still, nothing cured her! Her days passed in fever and slumber- her nights broken between the white walls of the grim hospital. The fever- the cursed fever never went away! Sometimes she said something, she murmured in her sleep, but nobody understood what she said!

Government hospitals have endless patients coming in; not a single spot can be occupied for too long. Depressed, sleepy, her family had to take her home. High, vicious and diabolical- the fever remained with her- the fever that kept her asleep, a fever from which she never got up. She could barely open her eyes. Fragile and helpless- she became weak! It was painful to look at her! To set eyes on her on a dread of itself!

One day, however, her fever went down. She sat up on her bed. Everybody witnessed a restless bewilderment on her face- a fear that showed in her eyes. She did not say anything. She just looked around, in search of something?! When the fever returned, she fell asleep again!

Gradually, as days passed, she became afraid of everything. The fear grew day by day, but she never said why. She became withdrawn, alone, she crumbled with fear when anybody asked her why? The bones in her wrist shivered! She wanted to say something, but she could not say it. "Did anything happen at the hospital?" her mother asked, her father ask. They asked the same question over and over again, but all she replied was, "Nothing." She said this after a lot of struggle within herself. A tear or two dripped writhing from her eyes- the terrorised eyes of her repulsed with dismay and loss!

Everybody tried a lot, but she stopped eating one day. The fear- the distress most unknown and insidious, broke her from inside- broke her inside! A condition most contorting- *the eater of bones took her nowhere*! Her people could only watch her break, a sight most devastating ruined their days and nights! She was taken to a psychiatrist, but he too could not help! They tried to force-feed her but failed miserably. Her hands got stiff! Her jaws straighter. She looked at everyone in horror! Sometimes, with self-desperation, she moved her lips to say something, but in vain!

Poverty, sickness and debt worsened their state- a different threat loomed over their heads now. The woman's family started thinking of her condition as no longer a disease but something else! Their worries started mounting. When they questioned her for her own good (to save her life), she remained quiet at first. Her eyes sank deep inside her black sockets- her black eyes reduced to shredded, morbid, rendered by sleepless nights! She mumbled something, but no words came out of her. When she finally spoke, only the remnants of her last words came out, but were indecipherable! So, she sat down and started crying. Her mother told everyone to go out of the room. She urged her frightened daughter to speak to her frightened daughter alone in person!

When everybody left, her mother asked her, "What are you scared of so much? Tell me!"

She looked at her mother with two fearfully terrified eyes. Then, all the sanctity of the human soul storms out, waning out, getting lost in ominous winds of torturous darkness of what she says next! She said, "I want to say, but *they* do not let me speak!"

Her mother caught her cold hands, frightened, she asked, "They? Who? Who!"

With her throat swollen with fear, her black eyes red- wreaking terror, she tightly clasps her mother's hands back. Then, with her forehead furrows arched (perspiring broodingly!) she tells her mother about the woman she saw in the hospital bathroom (what she said is still unknown!). Her mother starts to shiver- her hands trembling, contorting cold in a chilling haggard! Unfortunately, it is not this revulsion that reveals the interior- enskinning the physical to an *appalling bleak* but what she *says* then! What she says then unlocks a Rory– it opens a door to a cruel fantasy of some savage civilisation! A place where death does not die- rather it deforms- rots, giving birth to something even more brutally terrifying! "I've always wanted to tell you this!" said she, "*But whenever I went to say it, countless hands came fluttering at me through the window!! A red speck of light fell on my forehead from somewhere! A horrible pain – a hurting most grimacing grew unbearable inside my head! They! Those hands silenced me- shutting my lips- making me fall asleep!!*" Her eyes were mortified as she spoke what remained in her.

An *Ojha* was called immediately to their house. Several rituals were performed to dispossess her- a lot of rites! But maybe it was too late, she died the next day.

THE HEXE

Hilda lived in a rugged cottage. She lived alone with her herbs and cotton balls, making red and black extracts all day. She called them *Tränke* while the "other" (the *Dörfler*) saw her potions as poisons and her a witch! A pot of two cooked in her eldritch cottage, a fume or two always came out! These strange doings of hers kept her away from the *die Dörfler*. She was a bad omen, a walking curse- a demoness living in her grim cottage. "Death bringer, black witch, blood drinker!" they shouted, they threw dung at her- spitting in her path.

Hilda however, lost in her own world, boiled herbs and insects – starving on days when leaves won't bear fruits. The children romping around her cottage threw stones at her. They too called her the *Hexe*. The stones and pebbles hit her door many times. Despite anger, she would silently close the door and wait until the black of the night would fall and she would be protected in the shadows of nature. Everything is a rage, a rage going through fire.

During daytime, Hilda went out to the woods to collect leaves, branches and roots. She went to places where even the woodsmen would not have the courage of setting their foot due to ferocious animals and dark spirits. Hilda, however ambled to whichever part or depth of the woods she felt like. She sang to birds, wandered between the fireflies and talked to animals. Lonely but wandering, her life passed studying the plants and cutting and drying them! Frayed tree barks lay spread outside her hut, and inside, strange flames of strange things rose – fumes that induced fear- invoked terror in the hearts of *the Dörfler*! They said, "The

Hexe must be onto something!" Some even said, "We must keep our children close, tonight may be the night!"

Whether the frigid cold of winters or the scorching scalding summers, Hilda went up the mountains in search of nettles, ghost pipes and plants that would save lives – lives of deer, lives of squirrels, lives of elephants who fell sick living alone in the lost woodland. Hilda was very fond of animals. The horses, the monkeys, the racoons and even the bears knew her – they never attacked her.

Hilda's hut was in a strange realm – the chrysanthemums, primroses and ox-eye daisies bloomed in her backyard, while the gruesome weeds and marsh were in the front. In this sharply distinct blend of reality, she cut the leaves of severed branches all day. Branches she then immersed in black bottles and kept them out in the sun for days. In the shadowy dark, the *Tränke* came out fine! Rows and rows of these black bottles remained in the recess, which, when she applied on gashes, healed them.

One night when Hilda was sleeping in her cottage, a sharp knock on the door woke her up. 'Who is it?" she thought at first, and then the thought of a thief, a burglar, a killer and even a ghost pervaded her. Then she remembered she is a witch after all - nobody will come to steal her! "But people might come to kill her; they already abhor her," she thought, her heart pounding terribly. She prayed to the forest spirits- the *Fänggen*, the *Hylde-moer* to protect her and, hiding a dagger behind her back, she chose her steps towards the cottage door.

She waited behind the heavy wooden door glistened by firelight, and hearing another knock, she unlocked the door! To her surprise, there was a woman standing holding a child in her lap. The child was little, had very few teeth, and his eyes were watery. The woman with her strange, grey eyes kept looking at Hilda.

"I am from the village. This is my son; he has been crying. Can you help?"

Hilda, awake and alive by a sudden jerk of a change, said, "Come in, please."

Then, in the yellow light of the hut's interior, Hilda pulled a chair and said decently, "Please sit down."

The mother sat down with the child in her lap, and the child was still mewling. Hilda sat on her knees and checked the child. The little eyes were red – a sign of constant crying for hours. Then she touched his belly and pressed a bit, to which the *Kindchen* started crying loudly.

"Maybe it's the stomach!" said Hilda, her iris flickering yellow in the fiery tinge of the room. For a moment, she looked like *Hexe*, the axes lined in the quiet corner of the dwelling. The woman saw that- she saw her *yellow eyes*, the foreboding tales of her lit, awake, coming to life in the cold 'bony' glimmer of the fireplace. The fire turning to ashes in the inglenook- the *Hexe* with fiery eyes now looked at her! "My husband is sleeping; he does not know I am here," said she, quite the reverse of what she has been thinking. Her fingers and heart turned to pale, barren as she watched the Hexe in the sickly shimmer. "*Kindlifresser! (*Child-eater!)" The name returned to her disposition, wrenching her heart cruelly-mortifying! She held her child close to her chest- the *Hexe* was watching him still- she who is insatiably curious! "I must go," she said, sitting up with her child, her body shaking with the violent *grausam* thoughts!!

"Wait," said Hilda as she stood up with the other two.

Hilda walked straight to her table shining by the moonlight. There, from a cluster of dark potions, she picked one and came running back. She gave the *Tränke* (which, to her decree, was probably the 'worthy one') to the woman and informed, "Give him two drops tonight. Four drops from tomorrow."

"Ok- I will!" replied she in a hurried flight of fear, trying to get her throat off the witch. Almost snatching the potion from Hilda, she, with her sick child, left hastily. Hilda kept watching them through her half-open cottage door until they disappeared into the rows of dark, tall palm trees behind the barn.

Some nights later, the door of her cottage was knocked again. Everybody lay asleep- the dark surroundings without the moon shed a darkness so profound that the fleshy heart descends to the gorge of depravity! In such a dwelling of despair, the lone door of the feared cottage shook again. When Hilda opened, it was the same woman. She gave Hilda a silver coin and said, "Thank you, the *Zaubertrank* helped!" When the strange woman left, Hilda was still standing holding the shining coin in her hand, a feeling very intense, so vehement caught her. She felt a happiness curdled with breathlessness. She oozed with a feeling anew unchained in her. All she could gush in her mind was, "A silver coin! A silver coin after all."

Eight nights later, five heavy knocks shuddered the cottage door. Two men has bought a bleeding man to her forsaken cottage. They all looked like rogues; they had guns! "Must be the *Wehrbauern* rascals!" thought Hilda.

"From the borders?" she asked.

The two shameless men nodded their heads.

Hilda stood silent aside, making way for them (She knows these fellows! They were notorious for causing unrest). Still, something in her crevasse kept her quiet. She was not afraid of guns but of sorrow that shadows human sins! They dragged the *harmed* soul and put him on the cold floor. Blood oozed from his knees, worse- the scamp could not breathe.

"We heard you are a witch. You can close gun holes with *Zaubertrank*," said one of the rascals, the dying man screeching with agony.

Not sure she could do such a ridiculous thing like closing wounds with magic potions, but still, she desired to help.

"Hurry! We need your help!"

Hilda saw for the first time there were not just afraid, they were desperate to protect their friend's life. The same desperation Hilda remembered seeing in the eyes of animals, "After all, everybody wants to be saved!" she thought.

"When was he shot?" asked the *Hexe*.

"About half an hour back," replied the men.

"Is he shot anywhere else?"

"No"

"Put him on the cot!"

Without losing a moment, they put the man up on the wooden cot where the witch *spelt* eagles and wild geese. She first put a dark red potion (that resembled blood) in the place where the bullets made *cursed holes*! The man twisted with pain- a feeling of strange silence reeked through the village night. Hilda then used a crude retractor and a burned needle to take out the bullets. Then, with a *Tränke* she prepared from burnt marsh weeds, she dressed the rogue's knee. The scoundrel stopped groaning within a while, and his two allies looked at each other with utter disbelief!

"You must wait, gentlemen. It will take some time for the antidotes to work. I am giving you something (she produced a *gin bottle with roots floating*). Make him sip every thirty minutes until he wakes up," saying, Hilda gave them *the thing*!

The two rogues nodded their heads on receiving the *elixir* from the witch. Then, drinking the ale the *Hexe* has given them, they waited for the sick man to open his eyes.

After two hours or so, Hilda was standing with the two strange men, giving her ten gold coins for the incredible thing done! The rascal has opened his eyes! Hilda, on the other hand, could not believe what she was seeing – Ten Gold Coins!! She has never seen such beautiful coins before! Such precious glittery things! She could not even gauge their worth; she could not believe her stars, the night. Through the cottage windows, she saw the two men leaving with their friend in a horse-drawn carriage. The third rogue could sit up now. They waved back at Hilda, thanking her again. The lantern of the black carriage slowly and silently rode down, getting lost in the mist of the forest.

The news of Hilda treating a man with a gunshot wound spread fast. Day by day, more people started visiting her, with different ailments, different reasons – more folks lined up before her cottage. From fever to mosquito bites, she had a *Tränke* for everything. The canisters of her potions doubled over. People started believing in Hilda. They even bought their cows and horses for her. She removed their ticks, dressed their wounds. Hilda found a place in the villagers' hearts. They stopped calling her the *Hexe*, instead they called her *Elixierbrauer*- the one who makes *magic potions*!!

BLACK HOUSE

Karuna lived in a village called Belapur. Her father Sailesh was a fisherman, and her mother Nirmala was a maid. Karuna studied in a nearby school. Although they were poor, her parents still put her in the village school- all the teachers praised her a lot. However, the headmaster often summoned Karuna's parents for unpaid fees.

In dry seasons of summer when the rivers dried up and the fishes were hard to get by, the family suffered a lot – little food, little money, little sleep and little everything. But Karuna was immune to all these little problems – she has seen poverty since her birth. All she wanted was to study and become a botanist when she grows up. All she loved was her books and sometimes, she also liked to stroll in the wild nature. Every day after her mother returned from work, she and her went for a walk on the fringes of forest reserve. There, Karuna enjoyed the sight of curly red, yellow flowers- the evening falls and dark nights very much!

One day, the gram panchayat announced the good news - Belapur was going to have electricity! People were overjoyed. In about five months, the electrical lines and the tall posts were ready - the connection was set up finally! While everybody came to panchayat's office to get for connection, Karuna's family did not. They could not bear the light of glowing bulbs on their meagre earnings. Tubes and bulbs were fairy tales for them! The head of gram panchayat himself came to Karuna's house to ask about the matter, but Sailesh politely declined his offer. Karuna's pending school fees, the rising costs of school books, food, water– he could not manage it anymore. Karuna however, watched the whole *current* drama through the rusted bars of her broken windows. She wished if she could have that brilliant glow at her home – it could have magically lit up everything!!

The village houses glowed with new light of electricity. The trees, tube wells, bazaar and the bus road – all had the that fresh spark of electric light! Karuna and her mother witnessed these fast-changing scenes sitting in the candlelight of their lonely hut.

Exam days rushed near, Karuna studied double hours. Other children went to the village master's home to study, but Karuna could not. They were poor, very poor perhaps but there was no time to lose - Karuna studied all by herself and sometimes, her mother who herself read up to seventh standard came to her rescue. Karuna had a sharp mind, she could memorize everything – from Maths to English to Science, she could grasp everything with her sharpness! She however sometimes thought if she could have that sparkling bulb in her home – how beautiful the walls would look!? Karuna's parents knew what their girl wanted but they could not help it.

At the end of the month, Sailesh and Nirmala went to the village bazaar to get their supplies - not much, just some ration, some hair oil, a soap and bunch of candles. They found everything but the candles. The woman who sold candles was absent that day.

"How will Karuna study now?" asked Nirmala.

"I do not know. People have electricity now. They do not need candles anymore. May be that is why, Buri Amma is not coming to the bazaar," replied Sailesh, scratching his hair.

"But what should we do now? It's almost evening now. We cannot go home empty hands!" jittered the worried mother.

It was true that only one candle was left for the day, it would last only the night. From next day on, they will not have anything. Sailesh and Nirmala went everywhere - looking for candles. No shops, not even the largest grocery shop of the bazaar had any candles. Skies fell upon them!

"What should we do now?" said Nirmala sitting down on the ground, holding her head.

Karuna's father watched the wobbly moon rise in the sky, the jittery night starting to fall. Caught in cruel fangs of a harsh reality, he watched the moon change colour – blue shades of the lonely sky rushed past the white glowing ball. He thought of something!

"You go back home Nirmala, Karuna must be alone."

"But where will you go?" asked Nirmala anxiously, a strand of hair falling across her deep, tensed eyes.

"Just go home, Nirmala. I will be back in a while," saying, Sailesh walked quickly and disappeared behind the grey pottery shop.

Two lanes, thirteen mango trees, two ponds and finally, the black-coloured house. It had a black signboard at its forehead on which was written, "Kindling Candles."

The door was open - Sailesh went inside the house. The dark corridor abandoned like a war tunnel opened to a room full of candles, everything reeked of hot molten wax!

"Is Buri Amma here?" asked Karuna's father in a shaky tone, the tiredness of a long walk catching up.

A very old woman wearing heavy spectacles came out from what looked like a tiny smoke-filled kitchen. The chamber has black bricks and black walls all around.

"Who?" said the old lady, in a calm voice.

"It is Sailesh, fisherman Sailesh- Karuna's father!"

"Come, Come, sit here!" welcomed the little old lady with lot of warmth.

"Why are you not coming to the bazaar Buri Amma? "

"Everybody has electric bulbs. Why will they need candles now!" sighed the old woman with sad face.

"Yes. You are not wrong, but I need a handful of it," urged Sailesh.

Buri Amma's eyes lit up- a million flickers talking through her eyes!

"You know our condition, Amma!" said Sailesh, heads down in poverty's shame. Then changing the subject he said, "Don't you want it, Buri Amma? The Electricity?"

"All my life, I have made candles. All my life, I have sold candles. Candles have lit my entire life. In these last days of life, why should I need anything else?"

"Don't say like that, Buri Amma. You still have a long life to live."

Buri Amma smiled a bit and then through the corner of her two little eyes wrinkled by ages of lonely dwelling, she murmured "Which candles do you want?" The old lady pointed to a corner where stood a pile of red, yellow and pink candles - some were sprinkled, some were striped, some even looked like candies!

Sailesh had never seen so many candles together. The moonlight sparkled on the candle pile like icebergs glisten in winter nights! Sailesh lost himself in the sight of little candle mountain!

"Buri Amma lives in a fairy's world," Sailesh thought, "A beautiful life indeed."

Buri Amma repeated once again, "Which one?"

Sailesh's daze broke suddenly He fell back to reality. His eyes moved to the right, then to the left, then on bottom corner of the last wooden shelf where laid sleeping was a peculiar blue candle! It was a simple one, not like the other decorated ones but strangely though, it had a horsehead at its top from which the wick came out. Sailesh pointed towards it.

Picking the strange candle up, the old woman bought it to Sailesh.

"How much for it?" asked Sailesh.

"What else do you need?" asked Buri Amma, ignoring Sailesh's question.

"Give me ten more candles- the plain white ones," replied Sailesh, thinking the horse candle to be costly.

"Thirty rupees."

"What? Just thirty rupees! Have Buri Amma lost her mind? Or is she shocked by the sudden loss of a lucrative taper trade caused by electricity?" wondered Sailesh. But he did not utter a word. He was a poor man after all- any little saving was a big saving for him.

"Thirty rupees," demanded the old woman again.

"Yes, yes. Sure!" said Sailesh, handing her the three ten-rupee notes.

Happily, taking the same route back – two ponds, thirteen mango trees and two lanes, he returned to the bazaar. The bazaar was empty, a pin-drop silence reigned everywhere. There was nobody, only the brilliant saffron of new streetlights revealed the new shining bus route. Walking across the road, Sailesh entered a maize field, it was dark as usual. All the way, he walked happy thinking his wife, daughter will be very happy seeing the candles. Especially the strange horse candle! Karuna never had many toys to play with – only a very few, that too the discarded ones of wealthy children in whose houses, Nirmala worked.

Sailesh was right. Both Nirmala and Karuna were extremely happy to see him come home with candles – their ammunition for the dark! They asked him many questions How did he get them? Did he take a lot of pain searching for them? Where did he get them finally? Answering all their questions, Sailesh gave Karuna the blue candle which she liked a lot! She took a pledge never to dispense the horsehead candle! It was too adorable to be burned. At the end, they were all very happy.

Another thing happened. A very odd thing that people of Belapur and other nearby villages came to see! The horsehead candle lit up Karuna's hut in an eternal oval glow, the wick never burned away, not even a single bit! Karuna's life was lit up, her house, hope, lanes, dreams scorched alight in the light of the deathless fire. The only person who could tell the mystery, Buri Amma - was already dead.

There is only thing more powerful than fear,
that's not happiness courage or hope but love.